TO Austin

Best of luck
in all you do!

Charles

LESSONS FROM NAILS

LESSONS FROM NAILS

by

Charles Kankam-Boateng

Charles Kankam-Boateng

©2023

ISBN: 979-8-9875530-0-8

Edited by Able & Willing Editing

and

Amy du Toit

Printed in the United States of America

ACKNOWLEDGEMENTS

To Dad and Mom, the epitome of *Put Education First*.

To my wife Theresa
and children, Lionel and Lillian.

My joy!

FOREWORD

I have always believed that everyone we meet, along the road we travel called life, shapes us in ways we often do not recognize right away. Whether that experience is good or bad, you take in that interaction, and it forms your thoughts and actions.

Charles and I only briefly shared that lane, but I knew very quickly that he was a man of integrity with a natural desire to serve others. The lens with which Charles views life is one that is devoid of filters, allowing him to see the person within.

Although Charles may not have realized the impact he had, I walked away from our interaction knowing he had provided me with opportunities for growth and would continue to do so to those he would meet.

Lessons from Nails does just that – it reminds us that we all have worth and that anything is possible as long as we believe in ourselves and in others.

Vicky (Morrow) Hutchings
Enterprise Business Solutions Architect
TN. Dept. of Finance & Administration - Strategic Technology Solutions

PREFACE

If life is a movie, make sure yours is not only nice but a *must* see. Lessons are an integral part of our lives; they ensure we don't repeat or duplicate errors. Comedian Trevor Noah said life will continue to teach you a lesson until you get it, and the ultimate lesson is death. My hope is you're able to pick up a few cues from *Lessons from Nails* and apply them before you exit this world, because knowledge without application is futile.

Many people romanticize the dream of changing the world. It sounds so good, but in reality you can only ever change a slice of the world and that is enough. We are but a blip in the infinite universe. Let's take a freedom fighter like Dr. Martin Luther King, Jr. for instance, he will forever be remembered for liberating African Americans from slavery in the United States. Although a localized revolution, it became a global eye opener that freedom was achievable and others followed.

The same applies to another freedom fighter, the late Dr. Kwame Nkrumah. He won a legal battle against British colonization, enabling his homeland to become the first in Africa to gain independence. Although this event took place in the sub-Saharan nation of Ghana, guess what, it started the liberation of other African countries from French and British rule. In his famous midnight speech, Nkrumah made a statement which ignited a fire that could not be quenched: *"the black man is capable of managing his own affairs."*

Let's break this down. The movement between two points on the spectrum, regardless of where they fall, has never been an easy road, but it is worth every bit of it. When you are able to move from point A to point B, you help others at point A to realize they too have the capacity to move. That's what happened in these two examples. Furthermore, you don't need everyone to agree with you in order to change your world. Name any iconic figure in history, be it in the faith or political arena, and I can bet you not everyone bought into their ideology. So let that settle in your mind and determine to do what you can, while you still have breath in your lungs. Remember, yesterday will forever remain an experience, tomorrow is a dream awaiting manifestation, but what you do today is critical because it can impact the trajectory of your life.

There will always be supporters and detractors and that's okay, move on! This book demystifies the concepts of greatness, success, leadership and the like. Most of these aforementioned concepts are overrated. Take *Lessons from Nails* and allow it to equip you with essential tools required to navigate life with efficiency and the right perspective towards the achievement of optimal results.

Who is this book for?

a. A timeless piece for all generations.
b. Mind shifters, knowledge, and growth seekers.
c. Philosophers and life enthusiasts.

Why this book?

I realize there are certain speeches and books which have impacted a whole generation and continue to impact people the world over. A few books in this category include *The Richest Man in Babylon, Rich Dad Poor Dad, The Power of Positive Thinking, Think and Grow Rich,* and *The Millionaire Next Door.* The power of books as a tool for influence cannot be downplayed, especially in this day and age of social media.

The purpose of this book then, is to serve as inspirational material. A social, or life hack, textbook in the hands of anyone who reads it.

CONTENTS

What's the one part of your body you can get into shape without exercise?

NAILS

And the story begins…

"An unexamined life is not worth living."
- Socrates

So, I sat down one day to do an introspective analysis about myself, nature, life, and my immediate environment. I kept asking myself, "What can I learn from my time on earth thus far?"

"Look deep into nature, and then you will understand everything better."
- Albert Einstein

For a surety, I knew mother nature was never devoid of her teaching grace and guidance, if only I could hold on enough. As I continued in this pensive mood, I decided to bring it home for every change first starts with us. So, I asked more personally, "What is there to learn about *myself?*" I looked for clues everywhere, then suddenly magic happened. My eyes fell on my fingernails and that was it. *Lessons from Nails* was birthed.

This book emerged as a result of that thought process. I realized nails are something we all have in common and something everyone can relate to, irrespective of age.

For the purposes of this book, when the word "nail" is used, the reference is to fingernails. When referring to toenails that will be identified.

So, let's go! What are some lessons we can all learn from our nails?

ONE
DON'T GIVE UP

I know this sounds like a cliché, but just as being a gentleman never goes out of fashion, this quote stands true at all times. "Don't give up!" We hear it frequently. But I mean it when I say to you: *DO NOT GIVE UP*.

Isn't it interesting to know that the entire human race has fingernails and there is not a single person on earth whose fingernails will not grow back when cut unless there is a medical ailment. But for 99% of the human race, when you cut your fingernails or toenails, they will grow back.

Family

A key area I would like you to focus your energy on building is your family. Don't give up on family, things can get better no matter the current state. Family is all we have. There are a few instances where people will leave their family's faith to convert to another, and in other extreme cases some young adults have been the subject of abuse within their family circle and have been removed by law, fled or been abandoned. But besides these exceptions not limited to what's mentioned here I do not believe there is a reason potent enough to desert your family or for your family to do likewise.

Sanity begins at home. Once the family unit is broken, no matter how excellent things appear to be working, the whole society is a disaster awaiting manifestation. Family bears the primary responsibility for educating and instilling good morals in children. They are responsible for teaching them right from wrong, good from evil, basic etiquette, ethics, and whether they will turn out to be discriminatory or not. These are common life skills I encourage every family to continue to teach. Family time should never be traded for money.

Large portions of Western culture tend to be all about work, making money, and becoming so called self-made millionaires. We idolize such things, but do not make the mistake of choosing the dollar over family. Family is one of the highest forms of wealth. To have your father, mother, grandparents, siblings, and cousins alive is a big deal. Treasure every moment along the way. Celebrate the small wins as well as the big successes in the family. Prioritize the overall health of your family.

Parents should endeavor to train their children to become responsible adults who will be accountable for their lives. Will you be able to look back 30, 40, or 50 years from today and say, "At least I tried, I did the best I knew how to?" Doing your best is not a 100% guarantee that your children will adhere to the teaching. In some cases they will grow into upstanding citizens, other times they sadly don't. But doing our best is all we can do to ensure they turn out right.

Family should be the first point to learn how to correct one another in love. If children are bullies or grow to be abusers in a relationship; if they lack self-worth, or have low self-esteem, most of the time, it is home where they learn these behaviors, sometimes consciously and other times unconsciously. If you grew up with a father or mother who treated you bad, this is not a reason to pass on hate, because two wrongs don't make a right. Let us choose progress over perfection in this area and never give up on family.

Job vs Career

In my opinion, career in this context has nothing to do with money per se. You will be rewarded to the degree of your perceived worth. I encourage the people I encounter to take their job or assignment on earth seriously. No one comes to this planet empty, so each of us must discover why we are here. Some are lucky enough to discover their talents and purpose early in life, while others learn later. It is important to seek these out, because until you do, no other substitute will give you true joy and fulfillment in life.

Therefore, I submit to you, don't give up on your career, whether you have yet to start, are in the middle of an ongoing project, or at the end of your assignment. As far as your career is concerned, you should be willing to die for what you stand for and believe in; these are the people history never forgets.

Your ever resilient fingernails serve as a reminder that even nature is instinctively telling you not to throw in the towel, so don't. This wisdom is ancient! For someone reading this, I hope this message finds you well. You have something inside you so strong, it bounces back every day like a voice from the other side of eternity. You possess a heart cry and there is an element in you the world needs before you exit, so don't give up. The end goal of a career is not to just cross off a checklist. Ideally, your work shouldn't end with you, there should be a succession plan in place, so your successes continue even after you are gone.

Let me share an everyday example. My big brother has stretched me on several occasions. Once, he advised me while I was working with the government in Nashville, Tennessee. First, he patted me on the back then encouraged me to strive to work for a Fortune 500 company. To be honest, that was not part of my goal at the time. But guess what, because I had someone to challenge me, today I have worked with a couple of them.

Nonetheless, there is a clear difference between a job and a career. I am not one of those people who are cynical about a 9-5 job. If you are called to work in that setting, go for it and give it your all. But, if that is only for a season for you, then brace for impact when you leap from the corporate ladder. Everyone is wired differently, not all of us can be entrepreneurs. Whatever your lot in life, make sure you love what you do, and that your mental health is intact. For me, the gift of writing is not a job, it is a passion and career.
So why do people give up? It is extremely important for us to establish the fact that there are some things we need to give up on. A bad habit that is weakening your health; a toxic relationship; following a visionless leader, company or organization; etc. In these cases, my advice is to get out ASAP! However, some people give up because they lack the motivation to press on.

I used to struggle with working out in order to stay fit so I would try to get on my treadmill at least twice per week. While this sounds easy, there was many a time I really didn't have the drive to exercise. You know what did the trick? I told myself I was only going to do a half mile in five minutes. Once I got on the treadmill, I found myself pushing to at least one mile, if not more, unless I was hard pressed for time.

I have since then discovered one of the keys to help you not give up is buried in the simple word "start". That may be all you need to do. You don't have to possess all the knowledge about a subject before you can talk about it. Speak confidently about what you do know, then evolve as you progress in your knowledge on the subject matter. Trying to figure everything out before you get started will only slow you down. Motivational speaker Zig Ziglar says, *"You don't have to be great to start, but you have to start to be great."* I would also add, if you don't start you will never finish. So, any time you are about to do the needed thing, but don't feel like it, remember my treadmill expeditions.

Giving Up – The Risk Factor

"The biggest risk is not taking any risk. In a world that's changing really quickly, the only strategy that is guaranteed to fail is not taking risks."
- Mark Zuckerberg

Many people give up their dreams and goals because they thought it was too risky to go on that adventure. The Wright brothers were pioneers, credited with flying the world's first successful motor-operated airplane. Imagine they had listened to the conservative naysayers who said it was too risky to fly.

Don't you think they considered the number of people who could potentially die if those planes went commercial and for whatever reason things did not work out? Each time they took the risk of attempting to fly, don't you think they were constantly faced with the threat of death? Has the world not seen the worst plane crashes? I don't mean to be insensitive, but to date we have seen numerous planes take off and never land, everybody on board presumed dead. Flying is risky!

I heard this first from businessman Jim Rohn, *"All of life is a risk; in fact, we're not going to get out alive."* Before you came into existence, the world was spinning, and after you leave, it will continue to spin. I do not mean to burst your bubble, but in the grand scheme of things you are insignificant. Hold on, before you say I disagree with this, first understand the angle I am coming from. Nature has a way of humbling us. We cannot negotiate with an incoming tsunami nor beg cancer to leave. We are plagued by external and internal risks. Even driving is risky – every time we drive, we put our lives at risk. Being the most thoughtful driver on the road does not guarantee a safe arrival, because a reckless driver can mess up your day.

Life is inherently risky, so what do you do?

1. STOP LIVING – don't do anything, remain comfortable where you are.
2. SURVIVAL MODE – do the bare minimum.
3. TAKE RISKS – this is the way to live your best life.

My recommendation among these three choices is pretty obvious. Take risks!

We all find ourselves here by no choice of our own. Our parents made a decision, and here we are. The Earth revolves on its axis every day, so why would you stop at a mundane life of existence? Embark on something that is deserving of your time. If you are not taking risks, you are not going anywhere. Those who play it safe most of the time, actually end up wounding themselves. As novelist Erica Jong said, *"If you don't risk anything, you risk even more."*

Embrace failure, because as you journey on the pathway to the top, failure is part of success. The fact you failed tells me you are moving. I love the way entrepreneur Jeff Bezos puts it: *"I knew that if I failed I wouldn't regret that, but I knew the one thing I might regret is not trying."* That should be the mindset of anyone who wishes to take risks.

I would assume you already know the saying: *"You miss a 100% of the shots you DON'T take."* I consider this a life hack. The point here is not to advocate taking careless risks. Your risks should be based on data, research, and instinct. When you know you are doing what is right, it is based on the right convictions and values. Taking risks solely based on emotions could be one of the most fatal mistakes you ever make. On the greener side of things, life has a reward system for those that take risks. Always remember the dream is free, but the hustle or risk is sold separately.

Giving Up – The Age Factor

"I made a resolve then that I was going to amount to something if I could. And no hours, nor amount of labor, nor amount of money would deter me from giving the best that there was in me."
- Colonel Sanders

You should check out the inspiring life of Kentucky Fried Chicken founder Colonel Sanders. Regardless of all the misfortunes that surrounded him throughout his life and career, he prevailed in the end. It is recorded that he started KFC at age 65, which means this happened after his retirement. Colonel Harland Sanders began franchising his chicken business with a $105 monthly Social Security check.

Currently, Kentucky Fried Chicken operates more than 5,200 restaurants in the United States and more than 15,000 stores around the world.

You hear many motivational speakers say age does not matter or age is just a number. Depending on the context, age can be an important tool but not the ultimate decider. Again, context is key. For instance, nobody is going to vote for a five-year-old to be the president of the United States. It does not work like that. Why? Because such a person, male or female, is immature and cannot lead a population of over 200 million people without the requisite knowledge and experience.

However, with maturity comes a sense of consciousness and being aware of yourself. Having the right image of yourself, coupled with a strong desire for change could make you dangerous to the point where nothing could stop you on your way to greatness. It doesn't really matter whether you are 15, 20, 30, 40, or 65 years old.

The Blind Side of Age

Age comes with excess information that becomes unnecessary baggage. It is typical of adults to take a lot into consideration before they arrive at a decision. We think about all the 'what if's' that could happen but not having to worry too much could unlock many possibilities, that's the whole point. If you have only one shirt you simply don't have any other option than to wear it every day. When you wake up however, and you have 50 shirts, then suddenly your decision making becomes extensive and can lead to time wastage, even becoming a brain drain on you. You now have to choose what color pants, socks, shoes, shirt and whether they match. Could this be the reason why Mark Zuckerberg prefers to wear tees and the late ex-CEO of Zappos, Tony Hsieh, did likewise? In essence, too much knowledge can slow you down because you want to get all the variables right before deciding. But as you sit idly on that idea, know that time waits for no man and time is money. Don't look at this the wrong way, a decision can also be made quickly with a lot of data. It is best to try and avoid both extremes.

In many faith circles it is taught you need to have a childlike faith and while there is truth in that, it's not to be confused with taking an informed and calculated risk. Having a childlike faith is to believe and trust without experience that everything is possible. A child will believe his dad can really buy him a plane if he is promised one. However, kids don't have enough capacity to process information before taking a risk.

The Positive Side of Age

All else being equal, with the right accumulation of knowledge combined with experience, one can use this to their advantage, especially when you consider the network you have built over the years.

Age can be a powerful tool overall because with age comes wisdom. Over time you meet lots of people on your way up, these people can play a major role depending on what you do with them. Don't confuse this with using people, but we can all agree there are times and places we need and can use a helping hand. Despite the disadvantages of being young, don't let anybody look down on you because of your age, rather challenge yourself to climb higher.

Giving Up – Common Sense Factor

If you were Thomas Edison, I bet you wouldn't try to invent the light bulb after 999 fails. Common sense would tell you to stop wasting your time after a couple of tries. Yes, over the years common sense has been a major blocker to some of the best inventions perhaps the world would have witnessed. What's the catch here? To become a trail blazer and a pacesetter, more often than not, we have to defy or go against common sense.

Giving Up – The Now Factor

One thing to keep in mind is what the philosophers call sub specie aeternitatis (Latin for 'under the aspect of eternity'). In other words, we are to consider the present in light of the eternal or long term. We might not see the end of the tunnel in the present, but we know there is light at the end of the tunnel for sure. It will take what we are doing in the now, on a consistent basis, to get us there. So, let's not get so caught up in the now that we lose focus on the bigger picture. The frustrations that come with every step can be discouraging, but we just have to keep moving and laying the foundation in the correct order.

Giving Up – Big Dreams

Having a big dream can be burdensome. There is a price to pay, whether we choose to defer it or to go ahead and just do it. If you don't pursue your purpose, you will end up daydreaming your way through an ordinary life, leaving a larger backlog for your successors. But if you mean business, then your dreams will most likely keep you awake every now and then when everyone else is sleeping.

It is my conviction that a dream that only survives one person's lifetime, was never a dream to begin with. For if the dream is worth it, then your posterity and allies will ensure its continuity long after you are gone. Guinness Brewery started in 1759. As of 2023 it has been in existence 264 years. Are you dreaming too small? Why not lay awake grappling with an empire size dream like Guinness!

Giving Up – The Debt Factor

Not everyone has debt. But if you ever find yourself in this situation, which according to the statistics most Americans do, what do you do? Let's look at two research facts.

Given the 126.2 million American households, the average household has around $8,161 in revolving debt, approximately $6,577 of which is credit card debt. With nearly 248 million Americans over the age of 18, that comes out to a total of $3,353 in credit card balances per US adult. This research is scary. It means you're likely to die with some form of debt to your name. Most people do. In fact, according to data provided to Credit.com by the credit bureau Experian, in December 2016, 73% of consumers had outstanding debt when they were reported as dead. Consumers carried an average total balance of $61,554, including mortgage debt. Excluding home loans, the average balance was $12,875 based on Experian's FileOne database, which includes 220 million consumers.

So, what do you do? Owing or having debt certainly does not, and should not, stop you from realizing your dreams no matter how big the debt is. Comedian Steve Harvey said *"If you're going through hell, keep going. Why would you stop in hell?"* Eventually you would have to come out and that's what you should strive for.

As powerful as money is, it is at the mercy of ideas. It can only thrive on what you choose to let it thrive on. I know of some big names who advocate prioritizing your debt. They stress becoming debt free before enjoying financial freedom. While there is wisdom in that, my challenge is, I don't see why I would work so hard to pay off $100k in debt, then start saving from the ground up, when I can invest $50k in a safe stock or mutual fund that could double and pay off the debt (This is not a financial advice, please consult with your financial advisor before making any financial decision). What you choose to do with your money is up to you. There are so many ways to invest, think through your options and apply wisdom.

The philosophy here is, do not focus too much on your debt, instead, think of making an investment that can pay off your debt. The goal should be to build a system that can help you save and invest concurrently.

While borrowing for startups may not always be the best route, if it has potential and you believe there is a high demand for your product or service based on your feasibility studies, then give it a shot. Many people think, "What if it doesn't work?" Well, what if it does work? No risk, no reward. Continue to sow seeds as long as you breathe. Priest and theologian Martin Luther said, *"Even if I knew that tomorrow the world would go to pieces, I would still plant my apple tree."*

Giving Up – Believe in Yourself

"The most important person to believe in you is YOU. Everyone else who believes in you means nothing, unless you believe in yourself."
- Patrick Bet-David

There is a story about a young marathon runner that uplifts the human spirit to believe in oneself and country. A story of a heroic battler who refused to let himself nor his home country down. In 1968 John Stephen Akhwari, a Tanzanian athlete, joined the Olympic Games held in Mexico. Akhwari accidentally bumped into another runner, took a horrific fall, and smashed his knee and shoulder on the pavement. This occurred less than halfway into the 42km race. With a dislocated knee, he slowly and gradually continued the race while bleeding and in extreme pain. He ran until he crossed the line a little over an hour after the winner of the marathon had finished. While many spectators had already left, his feat dazzled those who remained to watch the conclusion of the race. They began to cheer him on as he completed the course in last place behind the 57 other competitors. When the media finally got to him, they were very curious to know why he continued the race. He humbly replied, *"My country did not send me 5,000 miles to start the race. They sent me 5,000 miles to finish the race"*. Today, Akhwari's courageous finish is still rated as one of the most powerful sporting moments of all time, while the name of the winner is barely known. Akhwari finished what he had set out to do, and you can too when you believe in yourself.

The moment you believe in yourself, magic happens. It is almost as if you suddenly have all the energy in the world to do what you are called to do, so don't give up on yourself. The human will is very powerful in the sense that once the mind is made up, absolutely nothing can stop it.

President Kennedy delivered his *'Decision to Go to the Moon'* speech on May 25, 1961, before Congress. President Kennedy asked Dr. Wernher von Braun, the Director of the Marshall Space Flight Center from 1960 to 1970, what it would take to build a rocket able to transport man to the moon and back safely? Dr von Braun answered in five words: *"The will to do it"*. A committed decision is all it takes. Five years later, we landed on the moon. I use the word "we" because this is exactly what Kennedy meant when he told Congress, *"In a very real sense it will not be one man going to the moon, it will be an entire nation. For all of us must work to put him there."*

This would also explain why we believe that the most powerful nation actually exists in our mind, because the world has not yet seen it. Rather it is still locked up in our imagination (imagine – nation). The world needs 'imagineers' who won't stop at imagining, but will do what it takes to execute.

With my decades of experience in the tech industry, I have so much to say, particularly about the agile-scrum methodology. Many companies have a wish list of features they want to develop, but implementation does not come cheaply. I've realized over the years what has always worked has been unity within the team and their commitment to see it happen, even when the end product doesn't come out in the finest of shape. And that's okay, because in a scrum environment the goal is to develop the product and ship it out for users to interact with it. Perfection is not required for success. Even the best of tech companies like Apple, Facebook, Amazon, Alibaba and Microsoft, all continue to release software updates or patches to fix bugs or enhance their products, week in and week out.

Giving Up – The Perfectionist Syndrome

As initially stated, the purpose of the agile-scrum methodology is to release a version of the product with just enough usable features so early customers can then provide feedback for future product development (potentially shippable state). The focus is to get started with a workable product, then enhance and perfect it later. What sometimes happens when teams go after perfection is they end up with bottlenecks that eventually cause them to give up on their product. Can you think of a situation that ended this way? It doesn't have to be in the tech industry.

I once worked with a man named Michael, who was a developer. Michael was a perfectionist. He joined our company and didn't apply the agile-scrum methodology. We spent a lot of time waiting on him to deliver, but he kept saying there was something else left for him to tweak here and there. Michael was an experienced developer, but his style of working was not a fit in our environment and he ended up quitting after three or four months.

Whether you work in an agile-scrum environment or not, be smart enough to know when to release a product. Unnecessary perfection can weary both you and your prospective customers until one, or all, give up on what might be a great concept. Customers will not wait forever, always bear that in mind no matter the excuses!

Giving Up – No Manual

Have you ever bought something you had to return because there was no manual on how to operate or install it. In some cases, even though there was a manual, it was unclear and after spending so much time on it, you just gave up and decided to return the product?

In my role as a product owner, one of the things I did consistently was create three documents: status, experience, and gap analysis. The goal of the status document was to define the minimum viable product (MVP), set the tone for where we were, and define certain terminologies. Then, in the event I was not at work, my manager or someone else could easily fill my position. With this document they could, at a bare minimum, tell the current state of affairs. The experience document detailed a beginning-to-end flow of the current system, identifying limitations as well as opportunities for enhancement. The goal of this document was to inform anyone who came along about where we were currently and where we were going. The gap analysis document is only applicable with projects that are transitioning from an existing, perhaps a legacy, application to a more modern technology driven application. It seeks to bring parity between the two applications. Ideally, the new application should not just inherit all the existing features, but should be an enhanced user experience.

I have come to realize, that when there is no set process nor enough documentation, some people will give up if they are not resilient. You can't blame them though, because it creates a lot of frustration when you don't know your way around. Have you ever heard this, "I wish they were here to do this?" All they are saying is, they wish there was a manual or documentation showing how to do the job.

Many companies have long-term employees with so much implicit knowledge, which is never formally documented, that when they lose those employees, either through death or resignation, it causes a huge deficit to the organization. The key here, is to initiate a succession and retention plan. While working with a former employer, I realized they started onboarding a couple of fresh graduates from college who were on rotation programs. They would onboard a team for three to four months, then move them on to the next team. The idea was for them to have a 360-degree knowledgeability about the product. Decide today what strategy works for your space if you don't have one because the absence of manuals and a retention program may potentially lead to some employees giving up out of frustration as stated before.

Giving Up - Being an Introvert

I would highly recommend watching Susan Cain's TED talk, "The Power of Introverts"[1]. Below is a snapshot from what I gathered in line with the notion of giving up.

A lot of introverts have done great things under unique circumstances, however, there are still millions out there who haven't been able to conquer their fear because of this personality type. Sadly, many give up, especially when they are constantly put in teams. While she is not advocating working in silos, she states there is a need for balance – working independently and working as a team.

Her talk also enlightens one about the journey to the west, that is, how the world has evolved to this day particularly in the Western world. She points out that the Western world seems to favor a man of action over a man of contemplation. Compare this to past days, when the focus was on "the culture of character" where people like Abraham Lincoln were highly exalted for being modest and unassuming.

Things changed rapidly by the time we entered the 20th century; we began a new culture that historians call the "culture of personality". There was a radical shift from the agrarian society to big businesses which saw a lot of people migrating from small towns to large cities in search of new forms of income. More people climbing the corporate ladder meant increased competition, and while loyalty and hard work was all farmers had previously needed, now qualities like magnetism and charisma were required to succeed. The focus was now on winning with people, influence, and the self-help books of the day captured titles along these lines. That's where we are today, she calls it our *"cultural inheritance"*. Her final conclusions were, there should be a balance.

---

[1] Susan Cain: The Power of Introverts, TED Talk, 12 Mar 2014 (www.ted.com).

Before You Give Up

Before you give up on anything, remember why you embarked on that journey in the first place. What were your motives? Don't get distracted by the extras like awards, recognition, positions, titles, degrees, and associations. These things are good, and we welcome them when they come, but the key is to remain focused and not give up.

There were times we failed in agile-scrum sprints (a sprint is a cycle of work allocated to achieve a goal), but even failed sprints became successful eventually. We just needed to re-examine our motives and reset our vision accordingly.

Building a Sustainable Business

One of the things we can do to mitigate or help us not give up in the area of work, or an idea we set out to achieve, is something I learned from Naveen Jain. Naveen, an entrepreneur once labeled by award-winning storyteller Jay Shetty as *"A man on a mission to solve some of the world's biggest problems,"* says to ask yourself three questions before you set out and let this be a guide.

Why this? Define the business problem. Is the problem really a problem? Some businesses go out of business when they finally realize the problem they set out to fix was not really the problem at all. Rather there were bigger contributing issues which had been masked. In some cases, it takes massive research and development to unravel it.

Why now? Is this the right problem to solve? Has anything changed in the last two years to resolve this? Are there any solutions thus far? What are the steps in solving this big problem?

Why me? The most important question to ask yourself. What questions am I asking that are different from what everybody else is asking?

Arm yourself with these three "whys" and there is no telling what you can achieve in life. It's really the bullet proof to not giving up on your idea.

The most successful companies are not only great at asking the right questions, but they seek to develop products that are almost indispensable to the human race. Look at Apple and Microsoft, place their products in any country and I bet they will sell.

Consider this question: Can we survive without clean water? We know the answer is no and countless businesses have evolved the world over as a result. If you don't know where to begin as far as building a sustainable business, here are 15 industries that will be around forever according to Alux, a company dedicated to teaching others about wealth, happiness, prosperity, and how to get there.

1. Food
2. Residential Development
3. Commercial Space
4. Pharmacy
5. Transportation
6. Fashion
7. Commerce
8. Weddings, Events and Funerals
9. Kindergarten and Childcare
10. Loans and Financial Services
11. Hotels
12. Military
13. Energy
14. Telecom
15. Waste Management

This list is to help you get started. Ponder it and see if any area catches your attention. Then see if there is a need or hole in any of them you can fill.

Success has no respect of age, creed, color, race, education, family background, geographical location, etc. You may have come from a disadvantaged background, but you certainly don't have a disadvantaged brain. We don't get to determine where we were born but we can determine where we die and even get to choose to be buried or otherwise, that's the story of our lives. So be bold, take control of your life and begin to write your story, don't let someone else write it for you.

Taking this a step further to a tactical level, a manager may ask themselves why some employees give up. Have you created a healthy and diverse environment that empowers others? The reality is, when given the right conditions and referral channels, healthy employees help to grow and expand business. Think about it, with even 100 employees who have a network on LinkedIn or another professional site, they can easily recommend or help you sell your company. They will do this naturally if given a working environment in which they thrive, are well fed, taught to operate at best practice, are heard, and have a great team to work with. Good people make a great company.

Leader Core Values

Communication and collaboration are key in any growth environment. Every problem has a solution which will undeniably come from the human resources you have hired, so do your best in your capacity as a leader to promote freedom of speech and collaboration. When you do this, it encourages your employees to be transparent about their struggles. This will only happen when there is an open-door policy. As a leader, you also want to ensure that Benjamin Franklin's goal to *"never ruin an apology with an excuse"* is rooted in your work ethic.

As humans we are all prone to error, so when you err lead by example. If you do that, employees will be more inclined to emulate and reciprocate. All other things being equal, if the compensation is competitive enough, there is little reason for employees to give up on you. People move on for different reasons, but it should not be at an alarming rate if your work culture embodies some of the core values shared here.

The Working Knowledge Factor

A man can never rise above his mentality. The truth is our abilities are buried within our mentality. In other words, the human mind can only grasp things at its current level of capacity. Grow your mind and everything else will fall into place. Our abilities are confined or restricted to the boundaries of the mentality we carry, so we cannot rise any higher than who we think we are. Where we are today is exactly where we think we should be. If you believe you are destined for more, you will rise.

Have you heard that knowledge is power? While the basis of that is true, it is not entirely correct. Knowledge itself is not power; applied knowledge is power. If you do not apply knowledge, it only remains information. Head knowledge does not profit anyone unless it is applied.

If having head knowledge was enough, perhaps librarians would be the wealthiest people on the planet. Some of them read a lot of books in the library, yet they sit at one corner for years. I submit to you, seek knowledge as long as you live so you can maximize your potential. Wouldn't you rather have 999 quintillion worth of knowledge instead of a fancy car? The car cannot produce anything. The good thing about gaining knowledge is should you lose everything one day, the knowledge acquired over the years (not another fancy car) will help you gain it all back. That's what makes you, and helps you get back on your feet.

In today's world a "literate" is one who is able to learn and unlearn, then unlearn and re-learn. It loops till the day we die – when you get a new revelation, let the old one go. Just like you wouldn't mix new and old wine, don't mix new and old concepts unless they work in tandem with each other. According to writer Khalil Gibran, the goal is to *"advance, and never halt, for advancing is perfection."*

Advancing is an active continuous word which means we must keep on keeping on in our pursuit of knowledge, especially when it comes to relevant working knowledge which can equip you to be unstoppable. There is no reason to give up when you are unstoppable. Author Carroll Bryant said, *"Growing old is mandatory, but growing up is completely optional. This is because every individual is born to age and die one day, but along the way we have the option to grow up."* I say it this way – growing in age is constant, but maturity is optional.

Everybody is Special

Just as important as pursuing working knowledge is the ability to overlook flaws in favor of focusing on the gold in people. Humans don't all have the same level of influence and energy. Human 'being' here implies we are 'becoming' every day. It does not matter if you are taller, smarter, or more fashionable than me today, "I am becoming…" Human beings transition through various stages in their lives. No one is born married; it is a state single people transition into if they find a mate. Do kids remain kids forever? No, the natural progression is to grow. A person may have a protruding stomach today, but with diet and exercise, their story can change. Nudge yourself and say, "give me a couple of months of healthy living and workouts." This is all to say, things can change. Time and chance happen to everyone, so there is no point in tagging people by their past. Because a man is a smoker today, it does not mean he will always be. Perhaps he was, but not anymore.

Imagine a world where we all looked the same. If one robs a bank, how do we identify him? That's why I say we are all special and diversity is divinely orchestrated. Thank goodness the founding fathers of America caught this wisdom; today America has become the child of every country in the world, gleaning wisdom and talents from all walks of life. It is always such an amazing experience when you attend a naturalization ceremony. To see many different races and countries represented in any given state across the country.

When learning to overlook flaws, the body is a good example. No one part of the body is more important than the other. As powerful as the eyes are, we do not eat with our eyes. The fact that the eyes don't walk doesn't mean your feet will not need the eyes to walk. This is what we all have to know – everyone comes into this world with a "chip" installed in them. The universe is good at churning out chips. Each chip comes with unique prescription. Prescription here means, "Prescript in Action." Implying your life's script is in motion. So, don't give up on yourself and don't give up on your loved ones because we are all special.

To say we are truly born a genius is an understatement. A colleague of mine once complimented me. She said I know how to convince people better than she does, implying that I was more capable than she was. I quickly responded, "no, we are all smart." A fish will never be able to climb a tree but that does not make it dumb. Find your genius and you too will blossom. My advice here is – never sell your birthright of being a genius.

Also, it is worth pointing out that life is about completion not competition, however you need to understand the dynamics of the developmental process.

We are all in the queue, whether we like it or not. While you loaf about, know that others are rolling up their sleeves to get the job done and life will reward them accordingly. The world is not waiting for you.

These are life principles that do not change. Stop complaining, and stretch. Change can be painful, but on the other side of pain is joy. Eagles prune themselves at certain milestones and in doing so they gain new feathers and extend their lifespan. Likewise, we ought to work on new feathers that will take us to greater heights. Redefine yourself so you can extend your relevance in whatever domain you find yourself.

Hack the System

There have been many times I wanted to do something outside my normal routine, for instance, recently I started my new company LionsMatrix with the intent to build leaders and overall self-development. Naturally I had thoughts like "you are not there yet" or "you're not enough." Logically, it feels good to wait until you achieve something big before you start something significant, but what about the experience, wisdom and knowledge acquired over years of practice. What's your definition of "something big" that keeps holding you up to the point where you have given up on your ideas? How big is that "big" and who or what defines it as "big". These are pyramids we build in our minds and this 'big' is most likely a mirage.

There is always a starting point in life, we call it humble beginnings, so don't despise that. What's the point here? I understand there is a place for preparation, however you ought to know when you have gained enough weight to begin. The point of preparation is not so we prepare forever. Sometimes all you need to do is cast a stone and watch the magic happen. Like Mother Theresa said, *"I alone cannot change the world, but I can cast a stone across the waters to create many ripples."*

In the case where it's not been done before, get excited! You have an opportunity to be the first. That was the case for Roger Bannister, the first runner to break the 4-minute mile at 3:59.4. Countless people have broken it since, but if Roger hadn't felt it was possible or didn't think he was there yet, maybe he wouldn't have become a name we know today.

19

Another example is George Bernard Dantzig, a doctoral student at the University of California, Berkeley. In 1939, he mistook examples of unsolved statistics problems for a homework assignment and completed them. If he had known no one had solved the two problems before, maybe he wouldn't have dared. Think about it, of all the great statisticians who had been unsuccessful, what makes you think you can? Perhaps arriving late for class and missing what the professor had said before his arrival was a blessing. Unsolved doesn't mean unsolvable. So, hack the system, don't give up!

TWO
GROWTH

Let me pull a string from the previous chapter. Remember I said when you cut your nails they are going to grow back? This growth does not happen overnight, it's always a gradual process. This principle is the same for adults and children. There is an adage that says, *"the biggest room in this world, is the room for improvement."* In essence, we should never get to the point where we think we know it all, because it is at that point we begin to decline. It's our death point. Always be in a constant state of growth by renewing your mind. There must be a continual refactoring of the mind. Always strive to learn something new. If you are serious about growth, build what I will call a learning organization; personal structures set in place to learn. The goal of this chapter is simple – growth is good!

Another lesson we can learn about growth from our nails is – nails grow by themselves. Ray Dalio in his book *Principles* says the first, or at the core of all principles, is that you have to be an independent thinker. The onus lies on you, and not someone else, to think for you. You can soak in all the advice and recommendations out there but in the end, you have to decide. You are the ultimate decision maker!

Jim Rohn stated, *"formal education can make you a living, but self-education will make you a fortune."* What does this mean? In my opinion, he was inferring that your pastime is the best predictor of your future. We all have the same number of hours in a day, but what you do with them determines how far you can go and grow. Decide to learn and seek growth. The good thing about learning is the more you learn, the more you earn. It's a simple equation – remove the 'l' from "learn" and the outcome is "earn". By the time you master your craft, making money will be almost effortless, so learn how to play this game well. Time has no mercy for those who take it for granted. Think about this twice, if not thrice, and it will do you a lot of good.

No Limits

Let's stretch growth a bit. There is really no limit to what one can think or imagine. We live in a realm of possibilities, particularly with the advent of the metaverse. Why would people continue to think outside the box? In this era, those who are going to be the real disruptors have no idea that a box even exists.

I wish someone had told me when I was 15 or tender aged that "you only prosper by the truth you know" or "your feet can only take you to where your mind has been". This is so profound to me. The day I heard this last saying it shifted something within me, I knew I was never going to be the same again. I'm not talking materially, that's the least of my worries. I knew I had caught something mentally that would become evident on the outside later. You can call this type of growth "the miracle of the mind." Let's consider a couple of these miracles that can happen to you as you embark on your growth journey.

Miracle of the Mind

We live in an ocean of motions. To get a desired result we simply have to channel our energy in a certain direction, and that's where the miracle of the mind comes in. Miracle of the mind means having a beginner's mindset that is focused on growth. We need to be in a place where we are consistently, and curiously, exploring what could be.

Self-education – inspiring one's mind to make sure every department of your life gets better. Because we have many parts to us, our growth should be multi-dimensional and multi-faceted. Someone might know you to be an athlete, while another friend might be coming to you for entrepreneurial advice. People will only gravitate towards the part of you they know, that's why it's good to be well versed, especially in your core skills. We need to know how to process information and issues, and how to properly manage or expend our energy. We must focus our energy on what matters and be patient, because building an all-round richness of the mind takes patience. This is a quality that will set you apart and form the foundation for wonders to find expression in your life.

Your mind has to be fruitful. Whatever you give it, it should be able to make sense of it in order to produce the right fruit outwardly and add value to your life. This can only happen when you have accumulated enough knowledge and wisdom to decide what has value. At that point it is easy to separate the wheat from the weeds in your mind. Your mind begins to operate like a sieve, it will let you know what you need and what you don't. What you don't need should go straight into the trash can. If a quarter of the world's population would operate in this dimension, the world would not only be better but safer too. People would possess and exercise good judgement.

Miracle of the mind will also help organizations thrive as burdens will be lifted off most employees and employers.

I want to end with this – you are not a millionaire because you have a certain amount of money in your bank account today. Rather, the day you hatched that idea and made up your mind to act on it, that's when you became a millionaire. That was your own miracle of the mind.

Miracle of Understanding

The miracle of understanding is having the insight and capacity to discern what's right on a particular subject matter. You don't have to know it all because sometimes too much information can create confusion.

When you read material, continue asking yourself:

- ➢ How does this apply in the real world?
- ➢ How does this apply to me?
- ➢ Is this for informational purposes only, a historical account or what is this about?

It's one thing knowing and another thing having an understanding. Many people read daily, but how many gain genuine understanding of what they read? Not all understanding leads to action. Forming a solid state of understanding is leverage, serving as a tank or reservoir from which you draw from to arrive at a decision. You may not arrive at a full understanding all at once; sometimes it's an amalgamation of different ideas and thoughts. There will be times when you grab hold of 15% of the information here and 25% a week after on another subject that might not be directly related. The knowledge keeps building until you suddenly realize you have arrived at an understanding. It's like trying to put together a puzzle – when it comes together, no one has to tell you.

Understanding can make you calm when others are panicking; not because you are superhuman, but because you are aware of all the facts and have thought through the possible outcomes. The goal is that in all your getting, get an understanding in matters that matter. It gives you peace and so much comfort. Understanding can save you from unnecessary breakups and divorce, it can also save your company from going bankrupt. Understanding works like common sense – although common, but not common to everyone.

When people have a shared understanding, you can tell by how they respond to situations. A classic example is the case in Stephen R. Covey's book, *The 7 Habits of Highly Effective People*, where he recounted his experience at a hotel. After having several different encounters with the hotel staff, Covey was blown away at how each team member treated him and handled the situation they found themselves in. Then seeing the hotel's mission statement, which read "Uncompromising Personalized Service," Covey expressed his amazement at their operations to a manager. The manager asked, "Do you want to know the real key?" He then explained that their mission statement was customized to their specific situation, environment, and time. It was slightly different from the other hotel chains, although it was in harmony with their main mission. Covey asked who developed the mission statement and the manager replied, "Everybody". Everybody, at every level (the waitress, housekeepers, desk clerks and so on) was involved in writing the mission statement. This explained why the employees would admit to their own mistakes. After spilling coffee, one of the staff reported himself to the manager so his superior could call and apologize for the guest's coffee being delayed. No doubt about it, these folks really understood the mission statement!

Miracle Of Wisdom

Wisdom, as we have come to know, is the application of knowledge. The more you apply, the more you grow in your knowledge base. Wisdom is a shift from head knowledge to a real substance. Wisdom is the stabilizer that sustains the civilization of people. In my view, wisdom should not be considered the possession of a select few, but of all and sundry. We may not all hold the same level of wisdom, but the average person should have a baseline and that should suffice. If you rise without the corresponding wisdom, you will not get anywhere before you start to sink. But if you rise with intentionality and wisdom, then you are in for the kill. That explains why a lot of lottery winners go belly up in no time. I do not think I am saying anything out of the ordinary here. We need wisdom to be able to sustain success. Wisdom will teach you how to order your steps, where to step and where not to step.

Question: what is the address of wisdom? Can you show me the street I can find it? Let me know ASAP when you find it. Just because wisdom doesn't have a specific location, does not mean it does not exist. Take wisdom out of this world and you will see how abysmal and chaotic this planet would be. When you go to a place you admire, where everything is in order, you are not just seeing a sheer display of excellence but wisdom. Your level of wisdom will attract like-minded people to you, so do a self-check. How many people come to you for counsel and what caliber of people are they? That's a status update on your wisdom quotient. Many have chosen to ignore wisdom and have suffered hell on earth. Wisdom may come with a price tag but no matter the cost, make sure you pursue wisdom and you will never regret it. Get wisdom, not just for yourself, but for the prosperity of your world. Who wouldn't want to be friends with a sage.

Miracle of Doing

Another dimension of growth is what I call the miracle of doing. The miracle of doing goes hand in hand with the miracle of wisdom, but I thought I should expound on the doing, or application, part of wisdom here.

The only way to know more is by doing. The universe has a brilliant way of rewarding doers. My advice to you is to be a doer, because we belong to a generation of doers. As you begin to "do", you grow in your knowledge and experience of that trade.

You can read all the books on pushups, but if you do not practice it there is no way you can build your muscles. There is a knowledge that comes by possessing an understanding, however others can only be experienced when you are in the mud – now you can tell the real texture of the sand, not what you read in a textbook. This is where you get to determine if the description closely matches or is not anywhere close.

The fact is, you can study all the books on surfing but try it for the first time and I can 100% guarantee you will fall. Mistakes are part of life, that's what makes us human. If you have never failed before, you have never tried anything new – it is that simple. Failure is the price of greatness.

No one will know you have a good voice until you speak or sing. The good thing about doing is that it liberates others. Doing is contagious, trust me, so be happy and comfortable in your own skin. I remember one day I was dancing and singing happily aloud in my car and in no time, it caught fire and I saw people doing the same in their cars too. The world needs healers like you. So *"Just Do It!"*

Miracle Of Patience

"No matter how great the talent or efforts, some things just take time. You can't produce a baby in one month by getting nine women pregnant."
- Warren Buffet

Life is a process with many different seasons. The universe will not expedite the duration of your pregnancy because you are a favorite of heaven. Sometimes you only have one option, patience! What's the longest time you've had to wait on a connecting flight at the airport? No matter how long it took, I bet you made it to your final destination and that's what matters. It takes time to build a great career and any type of solid relationship, and this is only to remind you that life will reward you for waiting on your gift or craft. It is amazing what wonders we become when we wait for the right time before taking things to the next level. Imagine saying the three magic words "I love you" too early. Although these are life savers, saying them too early in a relationship could cause a negative reaction.

Many destinies have been crushed due to impatience. Impatience is the twin brother of destruction. Do you know how many people worldwide get scammed on a daily basis through internet fraud because they were promised gold or diamonds somewhere in a discreet location? Do you know how many people have lost their entire life savings to get rich quick schemes, like high yield investment programs, that promise "18%+ interest daily rates" on your money? You know that's not sustainable, so why are you investing in it? Others lose their destinies through reckless driving. No matter how urgent that appointment is, it is not worth losing your life. If you have to apologize for being late, do that instead of being impatient on the road and in some cases endangering other lives.

Avoid Greed

When we attach ourselves to one thing thinking that getting more and more will give us the ultimate happiness and satisfaction, we find ourselves in the greed zone. I'm not saying we shouldn't be ambitious, but greed is not good. Some believe the only place greed is good is Wall Street, but do you know how many people have committed suicide because they lost everything in trading options or when the market crashed.

I understand human needs can be insatiable, but there is a place of contentment. Every now and then I recommend doing a self-check of your motives vs. your pursuit. To some, the monk life might be despised as a life of suffering, but I see a lot of good habits we can learn from them, especially when it comes to simplicity.

One of the most painful lessons I have learned with growth is to avoid greed. In late 2017, when bitcoin was popping, I ended up putting 18 ETH (Ethereum) into a crypto passive income program called "Monetizecoin". The programmers and lead developer were super responsive. They would take feedback from the community and deliver ASAP. I can't remember exactly how much I invested overall, but I think it was $14k - $18k. After holding it for a while, it grew to $66k. I had the urge to withdraw the money, but greed wouldn't let me. I even tried a couple of times, but greed would say $66k could be $100k. I believed the deception that at least $100k would make me happy. To the shock of my life, I woke up the next day and the coin had tanked, my investment was close to nothing. I kept holding it, thinking it would go back up because let's be frank, who wants to sell at a loss. But I ended up being a bag holder and the program eventually collapsed. I had to pay back $35k in loans I had taken. In this case I don't regret taking the loan, although I wouldn't encourage anyone to take out a loan to do something as risky as this, what I do regret most is the greed that made me lose it all.

Do you know how many people in this world have lived their entire life without coming anywhere close to having even half of $66k? We are living in an era where we have become so spoiled that nothing seems to satisfy us. I have seen, and read stories, where people put everything on a penny stock. Penny stocks are extremely volatile. They can be up over 300% one day and down close to zero the next. Our attachment to things might be different, but this is not something I would wish for anybody. I hope you take a cue from this life lesson and be satisfied with what God has blessed you with.

Don't compare yourself to anybody but your former self – it could be your yesterday, or even the hour that just passed. Comparison is the thief of joy. It is fine to pray for more, but always be content with where you are and what you have.

Again, nails take time to grow, so let's avoid greed and cutting corners. Instead, let us learn not only from our past mistakes but also the mistakes of others. Louis Farrakhan said it perfectly, *"When you see men fall, don't laugh, learn. Learn. Because you (are) on your way up and the things that tempt people to fall, you and I are not free from that temptation, nor from the weakness that will cause us to stumble and fall."*

Do you know of companies that water down, or substitute, what was once a quality product for an inferior one so they can mass produce with the sole aim of making more money? Can you relate to seeing a product you once loved but now don't, or you even hate, because the manufacturer has reduced the size too much? Do you know a company that earns a lot of money but are stingy towards their employees? These are examples of greed in different forms and sooner or later they may pay a hefty prize for diminishing the customer experience. The customer remains the king and they can fire anybody, from the CEO to the janitor, by deciding not to buy your product as a result of your greed. Let people enjoy working for you, that's even a blessing on its own. A good name is better to be had than riches.

Unlearn the Lies

As you grow, you learn to bin certain lies and even some once believed "truths". Yes, I said it – discard some truths in the trash can. There are truths that worked for a certain time and season but are no longer relevant in our time. Speaking of unlearning the lies, growing up in Ghana, West Africa, they used to tell us that if you sing in the shower, you will invite ghosts. Today we know that is a blatant lie, so what was the motive behind it? They said those things to prevent us from swallowing soap or foam while bathing, because it had the potential to hurt us. I had to unlearn a bunch of things when I set out to learn the truth for myself. There were some things I just knew didn't sound right, or sit well, with me from my childhood days. The painful reality is, sometimes those who taught us growing up didn't know any better; they were indoctrinated, and they simply passed it on.

In one of his speeches, the late Dr. Myles Munroe encouraged his audience to educate oneself, so you don't pass your ignorance to your posterity. The easiest thing for any generation to do is criticize those who have gone before them, but don't stop with criticism. Let the correction begin with you.

While it is true we can be anything we want, don't be deceived by that statement because it is highly subjective. I would never be able to sing like Michael Jackson, my voice is just not configured for that. The fact my mind has conceived the thought to be like Michael Jackson, does not mean I should start a music career. Let me be straight with you – some things are just one-time occurrences and thoughts. Let them go.

The reality is, we can do many things in this limited body provided we dare to learn, have access to the right knowledge and tools, and the timing is right. A lot of things come into play to make the dream work. Your willpower is needed, your skill, your connections and hopefully the stars align in your favor. There is only so much luck can do for you, and there is only so much we can do for ourselves by working on our dreams. What we do know is, going the extra mile helps increase our luck.

Nurture Curiosity

Always be curious; a curious mind could be one of the richest assets anyone in the world can possess. Question everything that does not make sense to you. You may not get all the answers you desire at one time, or even in your lifetime, but getting answers and solutions will definitely take you farther than you have been. This is how kids grow. As toddlers their curiosity heightens, they want to touch and experiment with everything around them. However, if care is not taken they can hurt themselves, so nurturing curiosity should be guarded.

In the tech industry we appreciate people who are self-starters. At the same time, people who demonstrate a willingness to learn and are curious, or ask questions, are also valued. This positive quality could also turn sour if not managed properly. For instance, asking too many questions could make you appear a novice, especially if they are things you are expected to know or can easily Google. A colleague once jokingly said there is no such thing as a stupid question, except the one you can easily find on Google. This is so true, especially in the tech world. There is nothing wrong with asking reasonable questions, but be sure to not over burden one person. What you can do is leverage the team; set time to have working sessions with them if necessary, especially when you are onboarding in a new company. Have you experienced this in your workplace or domain?

Also, as you grow overall, you will discover people have personal boundaries and sometimes you should be able to read the body language if you are becoming annoying or crossing a line. Avoid asking too many personal questions in the workplace when you haven't yet built a personal relationship with the colleague. You are there to work, not discuss family matters. One strategy I have learned to use is to first ask myself, "Is this really necessary for me to ask and can this person help me in the first place?" If you are not sure, then that person is probably not the right one to ask.

Here are four simple "curiosity" and "growth" rules I try my best to live by.

1. CONTEMPLATING... If what I am doing isn't working, maybe it is about time to change things up.

2. When making a decision, I ask myself an IMPORTANT QUESTION: will I regret this decision when I look in the rear-view mirror or will I be proud of myself? My goal is never to compete or outperform someone else. If anything, the goal is to outperform my yesterday. Recently, I have been curious along these lines... How can I be the best version of a husband to my wife and father to my children?

3. Never invest (or nurture curiosity) in something that is not DEAR TO YOUR HEART. We don't have unlimited time and money to waste in life.

4. YOLO! You only live once, so make each day count.

Breaking Patterns

Part of growth is to break negative patterns. First, we need to recognize these patterns, then break them by practicing reverse learning. That's how to counter it, replace a bad habit with a good one. I recall reading *Secrets of the Millionaire Mind* by T. Harv Eker, where he shared a story about his wife always telling their kids to go to daddy whenever money matters came up. The why was simple – she grew up in an environment where the mother would always tell her siblings to go to their dad whenever money needs came to bear. When he realized this was an inherent pattern, he worked with his wife to deprogram her from this mindset. He assured her the children could also come to her for financial advice and both of them could consider ways to make it happen. You can change learned behavior also!

Subconsciously, there are some negative traits we pick up from our parents without even knowing they are wrong until we are told. Don't take this the wrong way, our parents were not perfect, and neither are we. These traits sometimes work like a sickle cell gene –we don't ask for them rather they are passed down without our permission. Now it's up to us to do something about it. While we may not be able to completely get rid of the negative trait, we can at least manage it. If you have anger issues, realize you are not the only one and understand it can be managed. Or if your parents were risk averse, especially when it came to entrepreneurship, it doesn't mean they are weak or bad, they just chose to live on the safer side of life. When you try to break out, there is a high probability they may try to stop you. Their reasoning is not wrong, they simply don't want you to get hurt. However, real growth will require you to break such limiting patterns and beliefs.

Punctuality

Given the right conditions, the growth of our nails is punctual. They show up on time even though the process is gradual. I once read on Google that the fingernail grows at an average of 3.47 millimeters(mm) per month, or about a tenth of a millimeter per day, while it takes about 6 months for a fingernail to fully grow back if it separates from the nail bed (or motherboard as I call it). It will not reattach. A damaged toenail takes even longer at up to 18 months for full repair. The snail does not have the same speed as a cheetah, but it does get to its destination on time.

As part of your growth, I would advise you to be punctual. If a mentor gives you a time to meet, be sure to get there on time. It is better to be 5 minutes early than 5 minutes late. Your mentor will admire your commitment to growth, and if time and willingness allows it, they may even share more with you than they originally intended. If you only have a 1-hour slot and you show up 30 minutes late, that means you only have 30 minutes to learn. However, if you are punctual you get the full hour of learning time, which all else being equal, will lead to maximized opportunity and growth. So be punctual even as your nails are punctual, they do not miss their time.

When I say be punctual, I also mean be present where the action is, it works like magic, triggering something in your mind. So go out and get some fresh air, let the universe unfold before your very eyes. Take note of the sunset. It does not set at the same time every day, but it sets at the exact time it was designed to.

Age

A faster nail growth rate is typically associated with younger people. Age matters when it comes to growth. Do not waste your youth. Some claim it has to do with hormones. Nail growth is said to peak during puberty and declines as our hormone levels balance out with age.

We can all agree that young people can quickly absorb more than say people in their 80s and 90s. A study by Dr. William Bean, conducted over the course of 35 years, showed a decline in the growth rate of his own left thumbnail from age 23 (where his nail grew at a rate of 0.123mm per day) to 67 (when the rate dropped to 0.095mm per day). This change in speed was thought to be attributed to blood circulation which slows with age.[2]

While you are young, be a knowledge seeker, stay hungry and commit to all round growth.

Add

I have also discovered the secret of growth is buried in just a three-letter word, "add". We all start out with an even, or common baseline, however the principle of addition separates us into different groups, some ordinary and some extraordinary. Being extraordinary therefore is a byproduct of many additions.

Do you want to have a nice physique? Do you want to be in good shape health wise? Do you desire a sound mind? All of these start with the three-letter word "add". Working out, for instance, is a function of daily adds or additions we commit to. Like anything else, success in this area will not come cheaply. Physical growth is not random, rather it is dependent on predetermined efforts. So set an alarm to work out, plan your day to include reading, and block out time for meditation so you can be alone, then watch how you'll grow within just a couple of months.

---

[2] How Fast Do Nails Grow? Contributing Factors and Tips for Growth, Healthline, 13 Apr 2018 (www.healthline.com/health/beauty-skin-care).

Awareness and Exposure

Another powerful secret to growth is awareness or exposure. Once you have been exposed, you cannot be unexposed. I go back to my native country of Ghana sometimes. When I was growing up there were certain places we longed to visit, yet when I returned to those places as an adult, one word stood out to me – "outgrown". I had literally outgrown the place.

I had since been exposed to far better places and environments and as the place in question had not been properly maintained, it had lost the spark it had when I was younger. It was then that I realized our sightedness is largely dependent on our naïveté and what we have become accustomed to. Destiny therefore could be at the mercy of one's sightedness. If you do not commit to higher realms of exposure, you will be limited. One of the reasons I recommend traveling, if you can afford to do so, is it opens your mind to how other people live and do things. Different designs and thoughts are how we learn and are surely one of the keys to growth.

Financial Growth and Investment

My mother has a funny saying – if a rich man spends all his money, you will no longer call him rich. In other words, the rich are rich because they understand the three-letter word "add". The movement from 0 to 1 million is nothing but a function of "add". When it comes to financial literacy, we understand that it is not how much you make, but how much you save. That's the hard truth, although when you earn much it gives you greater capacity to save much, thereby increasing the pace of reaching your financial goal early. No one randomly becomes a billionaire. Creating wealth is intentional. You have to make up your mind to get something if you mean it. Put your money where your mouth is.

I remember another conversation with my mother in which she recounted a talk she had with her late mother (my grandmother). She asked, "Mom, I hear lands were so cheap at Kejetia," (which is the central market in Kumasi in the Ashanti region of Ghana, West Africa), "...why didn't you buy one then?" My grandmother smiled and replied, "It is the same thing today. It may sound small according to today's standard, but when you look at the money we made then, it was not much either." If you can't afford it now, you probably couldn't afford it then.

I read somewhere that the best time to have invested in real estate was in the 1950s. The best time to have invested in stocks was in the 1990s. The best time to invest in cryptocurrency is NOW. We cannot afford to miss a good opportunity when we come across it. What is my point here? That real estate or land you want to buy, buy it now if you can afford it. Perez Saka Oppong, a friend of mine, jokingly said to me once that *"the only business that is real, is real estate."* We will all exit this world one day, but land remains constant.

One of the secrets of wealthy people is this – they would rather borrow against an asset, than sell it. The key is to add, and in the case where you cannot add – then maintain it. NEVER SELL unless it is an emergency and there is no other option.

No matter your age, start your "Financial Growth Addition" today.

Relational Growth

A man's worth can be seen in the number of lives he has impacted positively. In other words, in the number of lives he has "added" value of some sort to. On your death bed, your job won't (and cannot) save you, that's why you have to make time to intentionally "add" to your loved ones. No one is indispensable in this world, not even the President of the United States, but when you add to others, you will be remembered long after you are gone. Make a point to block time specifically to call loved ones. Do everything you can to enrich others. Like we say, no one becomes rich without enriching others.

Did you also know that adding to your relational growth is one of the strategies billionaires use to make even more money? The more you add to your network, the more your net worth increases. It is said you will be exactly where you are now in five years, but for the books you read and the friends you keep, so avoid careless friends and be intentional with your relational growth.

Spiritual Growth

Spirituality is one of the main areas I define wealth. It is very important we grow in our spirituality, because the spiritual world controls the physical world. A great way to steward your growth in this area is a quote I heard from brain coach, Jim Kwik - *"Do not give your sovereignty away by picking up your phone first thing in the morning."* Why? You will be distracted before you know it. Whether you are an early bird or late riser, make sure you are diligent about your spirituality. I am an early bird, so I am usually awake by 5:00 a.m. From my perspective, this is the right time to plug into your source, to pray, read, and meditate in the scriptures, and in my case, plan and prioritize my day. Even if you are not in the mood, you can listen to some songs to relax your nerves. Good music can touch the very core of your mind and soul, energizing you to move forward rather than backing down.

The Afterlife

Have you ever wondered what happens beyond your time on earth? Birth and death are unique to each of us and our passage through life is a privileged walk only we can take. Watching my wife give birth to our first born, and hearing the claps that accompanied his arrival, I wondered if there was an assembly on the other side – a gathering of people, reading the signs towards the end of one's life, eagerly anticipating the souls departure from earth and ushering them into a new birth canal? Death is a mystery and the pain of losing someone never goes away completely, but many times we live our lives thinking we will be here forever, forgetting that we are only travelers on a journey. Evangelist Billy Graham was once asked by a university student what he considered the greatest surprise of his life. He responded, *"The greatest surprise of life to me is the brevity of life. It passes so fast."* This is a concept young people find the hardest to understand, he continued. Likely because death seems to be something that should only happen in old age.

Spirituality can, to a degree, be thought of in trimesters. In the first trimester we know nothing, in the second trimester we are getting to know who we are as spiritual beings. In the third trimester, depending on what faith you belong to, I envision being sure of your final destination after you transition. Here is a simple analogy based on something you have in your home – a milk container. When you purchase milk products in gallon jugs from Walmart®,

36

Publix® or any of the chain stores, you first see how big it is and consider if you'll finish it within date. As days go by and you continue to use it, you go from the first to the third trimester. As long as there is milk in the container, not only can you consume it, but anybody who visits your home can as well. Once the milk runs out, the empty jug is thrown away. Where does it go? It goes straight into the trash can or dumpster. The end placement is inconsequential, and no one cares about it. Such is our life on earth. Once you pass on, whether you are embalmed or cremated makes no difference, the milk is finished, so it serves us well not to place too much emphasis on the size or beauty of the exterior. Instead, place emphasis on the milk inside the jug, that's the real stuff. In this context your real self is your spirit, ideals, values, and virtues.

When people visit your home and they like your milk, they are going to come back for more. On the contrary, if they don't like it, they won't bother returning. Such is life. That's why I said the focus should be on the milk itself.

Concerning the afterlife, we may have different understandings when it comes to this area. Some believe in re-incarnation and others don't. Nonetheless, whatever you believe, make sure you are in sync with your source before your milk runs out and be sure to serve as many people as possible before it expires.

Giving

I'm mentioning giving under the spiritual on purpose, because growing up we were told that givers never lack. I may not be able to decrypt how this works, but it looks like when we give, we somehow get more back. It adds to us in different ways that are inexplicable. Your giving can trigger someone to share a piece of advice that will educate you more than your whole time in college. Your giving can inspire someone to bless you in a way money can never pay for.

If all you do is inhale and never exhale, you will end up choking yourself and dying in the process. Sadly, that's how many people live their lives. They are choking in an attempt to take everything in (inhaling), while never giving back (exhaling), signaling they would rather die than live. This is an illustration I learned from preacher Joyce Meyer some years ago. Like I said, I may not be able to fully explain the concept, but I know for sure that giving adds to our worth both spiritually, physically, and financially, and in most cases, we get more back. Physically honoring your boss with a gift can open the door to your next promotion. I mean giving genuinely, not strictly for gain.

Pastor Don Gossett once said, *"I live to give. Life is to give and not to take. The giving life is the winning life."*

Jewish people have giving rooted in their culture so much so, they teach their children to do "tzedakah" alongside investing as they make money. Tzedakah generally refers to charity, but the word actually means "justice". Specifically, doing the right thing by helping people in need. Perhaps one of the most common ways to do tzedakah is giving money to the poor.

We give because we are blessed to give, not expecting anything in return, yet somehow we are rewarded by giving in diverse ways. Did you know that a simple smile is a form of giving and the reward is almost immediate. As you seek relational growth, don't forget to smile. People usually love to be around others who are cheerful rather than those with a gloomy outlook.

Intellectual Growth

I highly recommend blocking an hour a day, if you can, to build your intellectual property. If you cannot do an hour, do 30 minutes. If you cannot do 30 minutes, do 15 minutes. If you cannot do 15 minutes, do 5 minutes. If you cannot do 5 minutes, try a few seconds. My point is, seize the opportunity, do not let a day go by without growing intellectually. I know what you are thinking, "What can I learn in say 30 seconds?" Well, a lot. Look at this picture. They say a picture is worth a

Source: *Successpictures*

thousand words and this one says so much instantly. See, you've just grown in 30 seconds!

Almost everything around us keeps growing, including nature; you regress at your own risk. Growing up, my father used to say people do not plan to fail, they simply fail to plan. The truth is, if we refuse to grow our intellect, we will become victims. Our world has seen a great disruption, especially in the creative and technological industry. Blackberry phones used to be the norm to the point where former US President Barack Obama sought permission to use his own while in office. Little did we know, smartphones with touchscreens were going to take over. Everything is in a constant state of change, including us. What if I told you – you are not the same person you were before you started reading this book. My hope is that since you began reading you have added to your intellect.

Knowing Yourself

You are a spiritual being having a physical experience here on planet Earth. You do not have to wait until you pass on before you realize you are a spirit. At death, our earthly suit returns to where it came from –the dirt– while our spirit lives on. There is a song entitled, *Spirit in the Sky*, by Norman Greenbaum that puts it like this:

> *"When I die and they lay me to rest*
> *Gonna go to the place that's the best*
> *When I lay me down to die*
> *Goin' up to the spirit in the sky"*

Dirt was previously mentioned intentionally. Ashes to ashes, dust to dust, is a worldwide belief that suggests we came from the dust. I too believe this to be true. You ask how? Let's assume when your mother was pregnant, she went to the farmers' market to grab some veggies and organic fruits. Where do you think oranges originate from? The farm, correct? Where was the seed buried, in the ground correct? If you look at it carefully it should not be difficult to see the cycle we find ourselves in. In the same way, what goes into our mouths, eventually is expelled from our bodies back to the ground and the cycle continues. Eternity is programmed in our hearts, and it is placed in the seed of the woman. It is the same with animals, that's how fate has it.

What if I also told you that you don't see with your naked eyes, you actually see through "your" eyes? What you see is tainted by your values, upbringing and life experiences, things that will go with you into the afterlife, unlike the tissue of the eyes that will decay once you are gone. Does that make sense? Life is spiritual, regardless of what you think. It seems like there is this science, or some form of divinity, in every activity on earth. I remember one of the managers I worked with, Venu Chaganti, once told me - *"Charles, every grain has a name on it."*

Knowing Yourself in the Environment

The human body has five senses through which we interpret our world. Here is my personal acronym for our five senses 'Small Size Hen Fat Trouble'

S- Seeing
S- Smelling
H- Hearing
F- Feeling
T- Tasting

Let's take hearing and smelling for instance. If you enter a place where there's an active fire, you really do not need a fire alarm to tell you there is a fire. One could tell by the crackling sound and the smell of smoke there is danger. Your senses send a signal to your mind, and your body in turn reacts to it. It decides, based on your mental soundness, either to stay and die or to run for dear life.

Let's forge forward with this concept. From the day a child is born, until their exit, the mind constantly processes information, consciously and unconsciously. They take in information, which over time transforms negatively or positively, depending on what they feed on. In essence, outward man experiences life through his five senses. The way the subconscious mind works has always puzzled me, it never stops working. We may not initially have all the answers, but I marvel at the times I have a question, only for the brain to work on it for a while and produce the answer. It supplies solutions the best it can when you least expect it. This could be as simple as replying to a text message that came through two days prior. The brain recognizes an unresolved challenge and just like the behavior of nails, it refuses to give up.

Real Growth

"Growth inside fuels growth outside."
- John C. Maxwell

Your growth can be perceived on the outside after a while, especially by people who know you. Most of the time I am able to discern the depths of knowledge and wisdom of friends in my inner circle by their language and choice of words. I guess that's why the Proverb says, *"Even a fool when he is silent is considered wise"*. Have you heard the statement – "He has not found himself yet." Self is something you create, not find. When you step into the arena of real growth, you won't need to be told. Author Jerry Gillies says, *"You will recognize your own path when you come upon it, because you will suddenly have all the energy and imagination you will ever need."*

Others may have gone ahead of you, but you can still create yourself. Attach some uniqueness to your craft. What makes you different from the rest? What do you bring to the table?

Artist Tamara Kulish offers a wonderful illustration and quote reminding us it's alright to be broken, we just need to be broken in the correct way.

If an Egg is Broken By Outside Force, Life Ends. If Broken By Inside Force, Life Begins. Great Things Always Begin From Inside.

Source: tamarakulish.com

Another wonderful example of inner growth fueling outside growth is the Maasai people in Kenya, Africa. Boys in this tribe are trained to kill a lion with only a spear as a qualification (traditional rite of passage) for manhood. But being born into this clan does not automatically make the boys lion slayers, a whole heap of training and courage is necessary and it starts on the inside. There are videos that can be found on YouTube showing young Maasai on the hunt. Upon seeing the warriors, the lions leave their prey and run for their lives. They only have a spear or machete in hand but just their appearance and the look in their eyes cause the lions to flee. Then the Maasai take the lions food home. This is mind blowing! Are these guys superhuman? They don't seem to know fear at all. Please note however that this practice, allegedly, is being outlawed by the tribe themselves now due to the endangerment of animal populations.

Danger   Opportunity

The Chinese are also fearless, to a certain degree, because of their culture. The Chinese character for crisis is represented by two separate symbols: danger and opportunity. This helps them balance their response based on what is happening. Perhaps this explains their global exploits and presence in almost every country. There is an ingrained programming and once the picture is formed in the head, it is hard to break it.

When it comes to real growth, there are five types of people from my perspective:

1. OKAY GUY - usually raised up in a systematic environment. They grow into their parent's shoes and eventually become like their parents. To me this is considered normal irrespective of educational background. There is nothing wrong with taking up the same career as your parent, if you truly feel that is what you are called to do. But don't be afraid to strive to do things differently or be what you want to be if your parent's career is not for you.

2. CHANGED GUY – this is one level up from the "Okay Guy" and similar to the process in which a tadpole turns into a frog. When going through its transformation the tadpole first loses its tail, then four legs grow, skin toughens and in the end it changes its environment. It now lives permanently on the ground until it dies. There is no further significant change other than they may now have some survival skills when put in water. An example of a changed guy could be someone who is first to go to school in their family, gets gainfully employed but gets drowned in the praise of people that they stay at the same level perpetually. When a past glory becomes the reason for one's death of aspiration. Another example could be when someone starts a small business but for some reason is not able to scale up but is able to manage it at that level perpetually.

3. TRANSFORMED GUY – What's the difference between the changed guy and the transformed guy? More like the metamorphosis process where a caterpillar builds a cocoon then eventually becomes a butterfly, the transformed guy experiences multiple changes and in the end looks entirely different to how he began. I remember when I was moving out of Nashville and I informed my manager I was leaving Tennessee, he looked me in the eye and said "it is time to fly like a butterfly". The transformed guy is able to evolve, it could be from one domain to another, or even from one position to a higher position but they focus more on themselves and not others.

4. TRANSFORMER - You cannot be a transformer if you are not transformed yourself. You cannot convince others, if you are not convinced yourself. When a transformational agent walks into a room, there is something about them that says, "I am here". They command attention or have a presence that is undeniable. The transformer relates to the adage that says, "work so hard that you don't have to introduce yourself".

   ➢ Transformers are usually electric; they seem to have this "electricity", or high energy, quality. When people with high energy talk, you can feel it. Even their smile is contagious and works like magic.

   ➢ Transformers are self-confident. Their self-confidence does not come from a vacuum but is knowledge driven. Transformers simply inspire others but may not be intentional about training. The time you get to spend with a transformer is probably what he has been paid to share. This is not bad in itself; it just depends on your goals. This might differ from one transformer to another.

   ➢ Transformers overall are great people. At the same time, I want to debunk the idea that you have to be a genius, or famous, in order to be a transformer. History has so many transformers who never made it to the limelight, and I believe you are one of them. Being a transformer can be taught, learned and is reproducible. Anybody with the willpower to make a difference can become a transformer.

5. SERIAL TRANSFORMERS: Are seed-sowers; they always look for ways to sow seeds in people. They have programmed their minds to live a life of significance, maximizing the smallest chance they get. Think of the power of a seed, you plant an orange seed and it turns into an orange tree. Isn't that amazing? Bear in mind, an orange tree does not grow by itself but draws from its environment. It absorbs nutrients, water, and all sorts of things from the soil before it springs up. Many people may have the orange vision in mind but then wait until they have all the required resources (water, nutrients, sunlight, etc.) before beginning, underestimating how long planting itself takes. Seed-sowers don't wait!

The ideal type of person to become is a serial transformer. Not everyone will become a serial transformer, which is okay, but by all means know that it is a process, so why not start now? There is value in your tears, pain and struggles to the top. Use that to impact, or sow seeds, in others. Be intentional about being a seed-sower or serial transformer.

The world runs on ideas. The right ideas somehow find a way to attract the necessary resources if one learns how to network effectively. Anybody who desires to be a serial transformer must grow their network in order to maximize their influence. But remember, your goal as a serial transformer is to raise leaders, not followers, which means you don't need people following you around everywhere you go. The water and nutrients stay in the soil, yet play a vital role in the growth of the orange tree. Let people be themselves, they don't have to do exactly what you do.

There is absolutely no reason for competition between you and the people you sow seeds into. You should actually desire that they become greater than you are. That should be the goal of every serial transformer as the reality is, what we build ends up building us. Isn't it funny how your son or daughter today will be taking care of you when you are close to the other side and ultimately making your funeral arrangements when you pass on?

As a serial transformer, be sure to acknowledge the contributions of others in your life. Think of all the different components that must come together to make an orange tree. Water plays a vital part. Water comes from below for the most part, with the exception of rain or an irrigation system. It does not typically come from above, so when you are at the top never look down on the very people who have helped you reach where you are. Take a second and say to yourself, "I am not a forgetful person and I am not planning to be." As a serial transformer, some of your seeds may die in people, some will fall on the roadside, some might even reward your kindness by hurting you, but keep the dream alive. Build a blameless culture irrespective of what comes your way. For every one that disappoints you, I can guarantee more will appreciate you. Sometimes, like author Seth Godin famously said, *"People are not afraid of failure, they're afraid of blame."* So ensure you have a blameless culture, or system, built around you.

> *Affirmation: I vow to be a serial transformer. I am going to do all that it takes. I am going to make mistakes, fall, rise up, overcome all the hurdles and hope in the end I stand to be able to tell my story. My seed will not die, my seeds will not die in my hands, and no one can take it from me. Today, I affirm that I have become a magnet because I have the right seed and it attracts nothing but great people, great things, great places and excellence.*

If possible, pin this affirmation somewhere in your bedroom, or office, to serve as a constant reminder.

Enablers of Real Growth

Avoid Quick Return Syndrome
As far as real growth is concerned, one thing to keep in mind is to kill the tendency of what I call "quick return syndrome." Start taking a long-term view on things.

Focus
Focus is not only a word; it is also a command that holds so much power. Many times we want to do everything at once, but it has been proven over time that not all human beings are good at multi-tasking. Going this route will not always yield the most profit, the best it can offer perhaps will be a little progress here and there. Focus is at the center of success. Personally, I

believe if you can live with focus, you will become unstoppable. Focus is only a five-letter word, but the demand thereof is immeasurable. Your focus displays how serious you are, how determined you are, and if you truly mean what you say.

I actually have a confession and maybe you do too. Can you recollect how many times you have set out to do something only to stop after a few days? What happened to all the energy you had from day one? Even writing this book has taken probably close to four years. Not that I was working on it all the time. I started, then I put it down because life got in the way. I didn't touch it for probably more than three years, then I decided to pick it up again and what did the trick this time was focus. Why couldn't I finish it then? Because I lost focus. I would pick it up, only to put it down again. The urge to finish it has always been there, but the focus wasn't. Such is life; if you don't focus, you will not accomplish your goals.

It is also possible to doubt your idea. Questions such as, "Is this even worth it?" begin to creep in. Like Simon Sinek, author of *Start with Why: How Great Leaders Inspire Everyone to Take Action,* encourages his audience – remember your 'why' and let that motivate you. Just get it done. Will you allow a mad man to drive you? You won't because he lacks focus. Teenage drivers are charged a premium for insurance because they are easily distracted and get into accidents. So, my advice to you is to let go of self-doubt and any weight that may hinder you.

That brings me to my next point, laying aside "entangling weights". The athlete's sport or active wear are light for a reason. They do not have time to look at their watch while running. They do not have time to eat while running. They don't have time to chit chat, converse, gossip, backbite, drink, smoke, change clothes whiles running. They lay aside every weight to keep them focused in order to win. Focus might be a buzz word, but it is one word I believe is underrated. I'm not saying we cannot have two or three things going on at the same time. When we learn to master our focus, we can be diligent and productive in building many things at the same time. However, the challenge is that not many people really have this kind of single focus. So going back to my point, weight does slow us down.

What are some of the things that can also slow us down and derail our focus? Anger! Someone can anger you, or do something to you, and you end up leaving your job or your place in a company you were destined for. Sometimes these things come to build you up, but other times it is just a distraction that sets you up for destruction. Again, anger can make you lose focus and at the same time anger can also be used as a test for your promotion. How you respond, not react, will be the decider. So, take note, ANGER CAN LENGTHEN OR ABORT YOUR DESTINATION.

There are dimensions of focus. These are not meant to be a single bullet that applies to everyone. Some may be applicable to you, and some may not.

➤ FLEETING FOCUS – This type of focus is used to get temporary things done, mostly on a daily basis. An example could be setting an alarm to go to the gym; this will help you focus and get your workout done. It could be anything that gives you a reminder, an Apple or some other type of gizmo watch.

➤ TARGET FOCUS – Target focus is slightly different than fleeting focus. With this it could be something you saw, or have been exposed to, and you decided you wanted to do or get a particular thing. It could take a few years, even as many as 10 or more. For instance, you went to an event and saw a donor donate $10K to a foundation. Then you said to yourself one day, "I want to be able to do that." You may even forget about it after a while but once it registers on your mind, somehow planet earth will find a way to bring it back. There is no formula to how it works but it does. A psychologist could do a better job explaining this concept than I, but I am tempted to believe subconsciously the mind does not forget things. The mind has an intelligent way of separating serious and inconsequential information and storing it for later use. It somehow knows what to save in the serious "must have or must do" department. Sharing some of your focus targets with a friend could help you focus on the task. As you read this, begin to think about some of the targets you have and go to work! You may be one step away from making it happen.

➤ SEASONAL FOCUS – This focus comes in and out. It could be once or twice per year. For instance, you may host or attend an event every year, which is cyclical in nature. Farmers all over the world know when sowing and harvest time is for them. Knowing this helps them stay on top of their business in order to maximize profit. You are either sowing or harvesting at any giving moment of your life. You can choose to be lazy, and time will reward you accordingly. Anytime you get your paycheck, know that you have both fruit and seed embedded in it. You can choose to sow it, harvest it, or both. It is totally up to you.

➢ LIFETIME FOCUS – Lifetime focus is usually imprinted in your DNA even though we sometimes think we can change it. This is the ideal, or desired, picture you have in mind for your future, more like your imago. Where do you want to be in life vs where are you now? Do you know what to do to get where you want to be? What is the image you are seeing now; can you translate that to paper? What happens when you reach your highest point, do you stay there and wait to die? It may come to you as a shock when I say this, but there are a lot of factors that fuel your passion to reach this destination. Positive anger, hunger, love, exposure etc. – all of these are catalysts. My final thoughts are, only eternity can reveal our true impact, and the ripple effect we have when we share information, ideas, networks, and concepts to make our world a better place.

I will only expound on networks here just because I want to tug on a string. Do you know that some people in your network are keys to your next level? That is why it is important not to despise anybody around you, great or small, for no one knows what tomorrow holds. Yes, you read right, do you know there are people who are keys in disguise? There are proposals that when certain names are attached, the door opens immediately. Dishonoring people can temporarily or permanently shut some doors, and the last thing I would wish for you is for you to lose your lifetime focus due to your dishonor.

While you keep this lifetime focus in view, know that as your journey goes on, it is possible for you to build up so much value that your name becomes not only a key, but an asset. I hope your lifetime focus helps you to become a national key and asset. There are a lot of names today we all love to associate ourselves with or even proudly wear. You are next in line! The good news is, when we are able to attain these heights, we lighten the burden on our next generation. As you may know, there are places that would easily open to you if you belonged to a royal family. A great name is earned. Invest in yourself and you will indirectly invest in your name.

> *Affirmation: My lifetime focus will one day make me a national treasure.*

Mentoring

The road to figuring out the world is very messy, especially for babies. It takes a long time and process for them to figure things out. Imagine a baby just at the edge of an escalator or staircase; if not guided or pulled back, there will be tragedy. This is where having a mentor comes in handy. By now we all know the learning curve is not linear. I could not find a better way of defining mentorship than the way politician John C. Crosby describes it, *"Mentoring is a brain to pick, an ear to listen, and a push in the right direction."* I'd like to emphasize, "…the push in the right direction." The most effective mentors have been there and done that. The context and situation might differ, but you can bet the principles for success remain the same. The law of gravity works in every country, so these truths do not change. Mentors lay out a blueprint.

> *"Everybody that's successful lays a blueprint out."*
> - Kevin Hart

Developing A Growth Mindset

Professor Carol Dweck talks about "The Power of Yet" in a TEDx talk[3]. She spoke of a Chicago High School where if students failed to complete the required number of units for graduation, they received a grade of "not yet", instead of a fail. She went on to talk about how failure demoralizes, putting the person in the middle of nowhere. "Not yet," on the other hand, puts the student on a learning curve, giving them hope for the future. This was very encouraging to me. Perhaps all schools could adopt a similar strategy and use a different word instead of "fail". Can we make "not yet" go viral? You have my permission to be creative and create a story line around it. You can do something on Instagram, Tik Tok or Facebook – use what you have.

Not yet means you can do it, you just need to put in a bit more work. My goal here, as Professor Carol said, is not for schools to change their grading verbiage overnight. Rather, when parents read this book they will have the right perspective when their kids come home with an "F" or a "Fail". Instead of saying "you failed," they will now say "you are 'not yet' there so work at it", and everything will be okay. Although, I must admit I will be happy to see some changes in the academic world in this area as well.

If many schools began to adopt this logic, we would see an improvement in grades overall. It would build healthy relationships between parents and their kids. Simply put, basic human ability can be improved or developed for both youth and adults.[3]

In a tweet shared by Aaron Nerella he says, *"As an Indian, in spite of going to an international school for most of my life I feel our mindset was made to be a fixed mindset, more like if you fail a test you were just considered lesser and not motivated to aspire differently. I feel if I was brought up differently and encouraged to think differently rather than just achieve that next A would have made me have a growth mindset. I feel so sad but I hope a growth mindset takes me away from this."*

A "growth mindset" asks where am I and where am I going? What are some of the lessons learned from the experience, knowledge, information gathered so far? Many people quit in the valley of disappointment not knowing they were so close to the diamond. My question to you is, "Why quit when you are so close?" Learning can get messy but that's the way to go. If it was easy everyone would do it! At the end of the day, your growth is largely dependent on you.

"You have to go wholeheartedly into anything in order to achieve anything worth having."
- Frank Lloyd Wright

---

[3] Carol S Dweck, The Power of Yet, TEDx, 13 Sep 2014 www.youtube.com/@TEDx

THREE
BE PLIABLE

Be pliable means be flexible. Our nails are a bit hard, but they are not fixed. What can we learn from this? We shouldn't be fixed in our ways; we have to be fluid and pliable just as our nails are. Although they are a bit hard, they can be trimmed to different shapes as we desire, or we simply can cut them down if we want to. Think about it, there are some things we grew up with and they have literally become part and parcel of us. Now so ingrained in us, we have to work to let go of them in order to climb up the ladder. That's how we grow; change always come when we let go. You may have heard of Paul in the Bible, he wrote 13 books of the New Testament. He said, and I paraphrase, when I was a child I spoke, acted and behaved as a child. Everything I did was in that operational mode of what children do. But when I grew up, I learned to let go of childish things.

Letting go is where the magic happens, so learn to do so. Yes, there could be some habits and associations you have to release, but take this seriously. It can be tough, but break those limiting beliefs, old patterns, even the spirit of things done religiously that actually have nothing to do with religion. Doing things religiously is getting into a rut where you do things the same way over and over again. Life does not work like that. Life, as we have come to know, is ever changing and we need new ideas to help us rise above and combat challenges we are confronted with. So, you need to let go if your desire is to break free and rise to new levels.

Cut It Off

Recently I stumbled upon some precious information about lobsters and their growth process. Since that day I have not looked back. It was such a paradigm shift for me. Now I wish all humans would go to the lobster and learn from it to just "cut it off". What I learned is, it is a risky adventure for lobsters anytime they move from their current state to the next level of their growth. According to studies, there is no set time defined for lobsters to hide from predators after they molt. Some say two months of hiding, or a little more, until a new shell is formed. The lobster is programmed by nature to accept this by default, it does not complain or whine like we humans do. And lobsters are not the only species who go through this painful process in the

51

area of growth. You can check out on Google the gallery of creatures that molt. A few listed are the scorpion, the African dwarf frog, the Mexican red-knee tarantula, the elk, and the German Shepherd dog.

Then there is this to consider – within the first five to seven years of the lobster's life (approximately the time it takes to weigh a pound), a lobster may shed its shell up to 25 times. However, as the lobster gets bigger, the number of molting events decreases. The adult lobster may only molt about once a year or once in two years. Regardless, they still go through this change process.

If we liken this to humans, our champs are probably able to totally outperform their old feats, rebrand or recycle themselves only a few times before they have to retire or die. However, if we learn from nature, I think we can do better because we have a magnificent brain. We hail such people, but looking at these studies I think the human species has a lot of catching up to do. A lobster may shed its shell 25 times! We seem to have this "arrival mentality" once we achieve a big feat and that becomes the enemy of our future success. We should never rest on our laurels. We must constantly seek new ways of being pliable so we can break our own limits.

The Fulani Story

A Fulani man (herdsmen in West Africa) who owned a lot of cattle went and bought a pair of dark sunglasses for the first time. He immediately ran home and led all the cattle back to the corral. He sat down for hours thinking it was going to rain. When there was no rain, he became frustrated at the unusual experience. Eventually, he asked the children what was happening? They replied to him, "Daddy, it is your sunglasses." He took the sunglasses off only to realize they were right. The weather had not changed, it was the sunglasses that had darkened his outlook.

The moral of the story is this – if things are not working, ask around. Others may have the answers we need or we may well be overlooking the solution because we are too close to the problem. In the case of the Fulani man, he was pliable enough to ask and afterwards he reprogrammed himself based on the information he received from his own children. That is humility right there.

As parents, we should accept that we do not know everything, and sometimes we ought to learn from our kids. Perception, programming, and orientation are everything. It is fascinating to know that for those who are positive minded, everything is positive. This is not because they are fools, but they understand there is nothing to lose by being positive. Yet there is everything to lose by being pessimistic. Pessimism affects your very soul and could also lead to depression.

You may have heard a popular saying of Bruce Lee, *"be water, my friend."* To be like water is to be formless, or shapeless, to be fluid. When you put water into a cup, it takes on the shape of the cup. So, to be pliable means to be amorphous like the wind, oil, fire, and water; formless in a way that cannot be trapped. That is how we ought to be. Do not be so rigid and set in your ways that you cannot let go and move to the next level.

This is how pliable we ought to be in order to fit into any type of environment, especially when we desire to break into a different environment. When we are not pliable, the opposite inevitably happens as described by science-fiction writer Robert A. Heinlein — *"In the absence of clearly-defined goals, we become strangely loyal to performing daily trivia until ultimately we become enslaved by it."*

Got the memo now? I have also observed something, anytime I leave my toenails for a long time without tending to them, they become rough looking and awful. The last thing you want to do is wear flip flops or sandals in public where others can see your unkempt feet. The same applies to our fingernails. If common sense tells you to hide it, then know something is not right. So, think of it this way, whenever we are raw, fixed, unbending, or unrefined, nature will find a way to hide us. Nobody likes ugly, they will see you and pass by, that's just the way it is. While cutting it off might not be the sexiest of ideas, may take some time off your busy schedule, or even make you uncomfortable, understand the upside is it makes you healthy too.

Lesson from Abraham

There is a popular Old Testament story about Abram, whose name was changed to Abraham. He is known as the father of faith in the Bible. There was a test of faith that required him to sacrifice his promised gift. Things would have turned south for Abraham if he was fixed and unpliable, however he was open minded to receive the update that came at the eleventh hour. The update was a substitute for his son. His task was to sacrifice his son, instead his God provided a ram as a substitute, so he did not have to. With this lesson as our backdrop, do you see the importance of getting updates in order to stay relevant in life?

It may surprise you to know many organizations are still running with outdated software. The software may still work, it may still be able to produce some results, however if they don't change their ways they may end up getting stuck, or to some degree, self-destruct. Just because a software program gets the job done, does not mean it cannot be improved. It is for that reason there are periodic updates.

"The Digital Broker's Playbook"

I was reading a book on insurance, *The Digital Broker's Playbook* by David Reid, and he said something striking about those about to buy new agency management software and what to look for. *"When you are looking at a software solution today, ... try to discover exactly what that software looked like last year. If it had the same features then as it does today, don't buy it."* It is important software continually updates. Reid goes on to say, *"If you invest in a company that is built on yesterday's technology, you run the risk of also becoming yesterday's solution to your clients as well."*

I find this piece of advice invaluable to the subject matter at hand, which is, be pliable. Don't just think of it from a company's perspective but personalize it. Believe it or not, we are all in the buying and selling business. Some are direct and others indirect selling. If you are a journalist or a public speaker for example, in your trade you are selling your speech, and you have to protect your voice and ensure your voice remains relevant or else you will not go far. So, ask yourself, why should people continue to buy from you if you are not improving? Does this explain why some people leave their friends behind because they refuse to grow? Of course! It is possible to start with someone but be worlds apart in a few years.

Reid also mentioned that today in the insurance world, if you are still in the paper world you are out of the game. There was another part I loved so much, he said with confidence, *"Mark my words, if you spend the next eighteen months actively and deliberately digitizing your business - no matter what the size of your book, it's going to yield you the biggest return on investment of your entire career."*

As you reflect on this, ask yourself do you have an online presence for your business. If you are not online, you are out of the game. So don't be fixed in your mindset, be pliable. With Google at our fingertips, potential customers will easily skip you for your competitors.

The "Be Pliable" concept should not be misinterpreted to mean that individuals or companies should change their vision if there is no need. That is not the intent here. If you already have a solid vision, hold on to it. If you desire to expand or update, so be it. The method of operation may change from time to time because it is imperative to experiment and adapt quickly to meet current and future demands, but the content and the end goal may likely remain same.

For instance, if you sell a beverage in a plastic cup and it so happens that plastic cups have been banned, does it mean you have to stop producing the beverage? No. It simply means you must find an alternative container in which to distribute it. If society has moved onto wooden or metallic cup, analyze the cost and move in that direction. As a matter of fact, you don't have to wait for it to fade away before you make adjustments. You have to be aware enough to anticipate future needs and trends.

Let's consider another common-sense example. If you are a wedding planner whose job is specialized in outdoor events, mostly at beaches, it is only wise for you to plan for the rain just in case. You cannot be fixed in your mindset to say it will never rain just based on weather forecast. Life happens!

Also, let me point this out that some changes may not be appreciated initially, but give it a little time and when it makes sense, it will fly.

Potential Dangers of Not Being Pliable

BECOMING STALE: Don't ever come to a point where you lose your freshness. Freshness here is used to refer to losing relevance in your area of influence. Don't be fooled by a few people, or existing customers, still hanging around; it is just a matter of time before they leave. Sometimes there are people who do not love change themselves and will tie you down with their ideology. You only have two choices; either repeat and become stale or evolve. It's your call!

DECREASED PROFIT: Following the previous point, when we become stale by losing our freshness, our value, or profit, goes down with it. Again, people will always go to where they are getting value. Let's assume I have subscribed to your YouTube channel, and you are a caterer. I subscribed because I want to learn how to cook a variety of foods. If I no longer feel you are satisfying my need, I am going to unsubscribe - it is that simple. Also, some people may not be aware that views, comments, and reviews are a form of currency through which transactions are made. Why do you think companies, restaurants, and various organizations quickly apologize when they see a negative comment or review? They understand the power poor feedback has to hurt their business. If you are looking for feedback from real users, you can connect with G2.com.

HITTING THE ROOF: This is the resulting effect of not paying attention to the red flags that you are going out of business. Listen to what customers, subscribers, and followers are saying. Constructive criticisms should be welcomed, destructive criticisms should be trashed. Be open to listen and open your eyes, or else you are going to hit the roof. As Bill Gates said, *"Your most unhappy customers are your greatest source of learning."*

DEATH: History has taught us better. Death refers to companies that have died, or gone out of business, as a result of being unaware of, or unaligned with changes in the marketplace. Yes, it is possible to go out of business completely. I understand this sounds like a huge penalty to pay for your recalcitrance, but again you have a choice until it is too late. Too late means you can't breathe any more, until then you can still do something about it. You can resurrect a dead company if you decide to change your ways.

You cannot stop competitors from rising on the scene. Even the best economies don't rule forever. There are so many countries who have had their fair share of glory but are no longer counted among the ruling powers. No one likes the idea of death. We act like we are going to live forever. The reality is, we are dying daily even as we live; every second and every heartbeat draws us closer.

Not getting the requisite relevant education in your domain could also lead to death. This should not be confused with going to school because going to a formal school is not the only way to be educated, there are a lot of online courses these days for specific needs including emerging industries. In whatever field you find yourself remember others have already gone ahead of you. Learn from them, buy their books, connect with them, email them and travel to speak with them if you have to. Do what it takes to pursue knowledge. It gives you an advantage over others who refuse to be equipped.

Circumcision of the Mind

A key to staying pliable is circumcision of the mind. Every human being is rewarded with 24 hours each day, which is equivalent to 1,440 minutes each day. There is no special intelligence needed to know that time is a common denominator we all share. From the most educated man to the least, rich or poor, people of low or high rank, everyone has the same amount of time in a day.

The separator then is what I call the "circumcision of the mind." Thomas C. Corley, author of *Rich Habits - The Daily Success Habits of Wealthy Individuals,* outlines ten principles of "rich habits" established by interviewing 233 wealthy and 128 poor individuals over a span of three years, from March 2004 to March 2007. He then realized the self-made rich make good use of 240 of their minutes (4 hours) and this is what separates them from everyone else. 240 minutes are usually spent in the following areas: dream setting (pursuing their goals), deliberate practice or education, building relationships, and aerobic exercises.

Of course, you can't make money on a death bed in a hospital. Every minute counts and the times we spend being productive pays dividends down the road in diverse forms. Examples include virtuoso skills and knowledge, great health, all round wisdom, knowing how to apply and spend knowledge, greater network, and wealth. I hope you are able to "circumcise your mind" from the following areas, and by doing so, you can get more focused time to learn as you commit to a life of being pliable.

From my observation I believe another major area we need to circumcise is managing the time we spend on our phones and social media. They are not bad in themselves, both are great tools, however if not properly managed they can slow us down. You have no idea how mobile phone distractions are costing people a fortune every day. When I started working in the United States, I could clearly tell people who were diligent from those who weren't. I have worked with people who come to work and immediately turn their phones face down to avoid the distraction of looking at notifications. They would only pick up their phones for incoming calls or when they were expecting an important message. I quickly learned from them. This is something you can also do, but it is a choice. You can mute your phone or put it on vibrate, whatever works for you when you are at work. Whichever way you choose, be sure to block some time for yourself in the course of the day outside your work time.

I recall another time our manager sent us the results of conducted research about how distraction causes a lot of downtime among employees during working hours. It informed, when we get distracted while working, it can steal at least 20 minutes of manhours per day. It starts by just looking at a message, then before you realize it, one thing leads to another and another and by the time you finally realize you are not working and need to call it quits, 20 minutes may have elapsed.

We used to talk about mobile phone distractions in our scrum meetings. In those days we adopted agile during our retrospective analysis meetings. Retrospective meetings were meetings where we reflected on the process, identifying what went well, what did not go well and opportunities for improvement in the coming sprints. One of the suggestions was to keep our phones away during our daily scrum meetings because they were a distraction. Scrum only lasted 15 minutes and we could not afford to be distracted. We made it a rule not to check emails unless there was a need for someone to forward an email, read a passage, or call something out to the group.

Social media is also a distraction. This is not a campaign against any particular social media app but a genuine concern for the impact social media has had on the human race in depriving us of good sleep, increasing stress levels, causing unnecessary competition, and fueling depression, fear, and panic.

This is also an area that has caused many accidents on the road because someone was busy doing a live video while driving or holding their phone instead of the wheel. Since the inception of iPhones in 2007, the adoption and addiction rate has steadily grown to the point where today we are literally glued to these devices.

For some people, to go days without a mobile phone is like losing their blood. People get depressed and a few go to the extreme of committing suicide because they didn't feel loved based on little to no reactions to their post. According to SlickText article dated January 4th, 2022, the majority of Americans look at their phones up to 63 times per day to check email, texts, Facebook, Instagram, and other sites and apps.

Mobile phone addiction has become so prevalent that we know the patterns and trends, and how to get the most out of social media with precision and predictability. For instance, it's been determined the best days to post on Facebook are Saturdays and Sundays. Posting on these days, individuals could expect to get about 32% engagement, followed by Thursdays and Fridays with 18%. Higher engagement typically takes place during the hours of 9:00 a.m., 1:00 p.m. and 3:00 p.m. Posting around 1:00 p.m. garners the most clicks, while posting at 3:00 p.m. gleans the most shares, particularly on the weekends. In 2020 alone, Facebook bagged a whopping $86 billion in revenue which translates to a loss of approximately $163,565 for every minute of outage. Circumcising our minds from social media does not mean we should stop using it, rather we need to find a balance on how to use it to our advantage.

Fight Ignorance

In order to stay pliable, we ought to fight ignorance like a plague. We need to evolve on a daily basis; don't leave your life to chance. There is no such thing as a free lunch anywhere. We do not prosper or increase just by the mere passage of time. We prosper by growing in truth, the more the merrier. For instance, if you find yourself thinking "one day everything will be alright," that's a great thought, I love it, but that's wishful thinking and it may never surface if you don't back it up with actions. In actuality, that "one day" is also waiting to meet you, however the onus is on you to make the necessary adjustments by taking the required actions. Progress, among other factors, is either network or knowledge dependent.

There was a time I lost my voice. I wasted a whole week trying to recover my voice to no avail. Then a friend of mine advised me to mix ginger, lemon, and honey into a drink. I think I made a Lipton tea out of it. I blended and drank it and in no time, I recovered my voice. Can you imagine if I got paid for talking? I would have lost so much money by just waiting on my voice to recover by itself when there was a way to recover faster. It took my friend's knowledge to expedite the healing process.

Follow Your Convictions

There is time for everything. Personally, I believe there is an opportune time for everybody if we are able to see it, because it may come in disguise. Evangelist Leonard Ravenhill put it like this, *"the opportunity of a lifetime needs to be seized during the lifetime of the opportunity."*

Trail blazers like Mark Zuckerberg, Bill Gates, Elon Musk and many more, all left school when they saw the opportunity of a lifetime. The advent of the personal computer, internet, social media, and crypto have led to the emergence of extremely wealthy and successful people. Recessions have also proven to be a time where a lot of millionaires and billionaires are made. Like Warren Buffett said, *"Be fearful when others are greedy and greedy when others are fearful."* When crypto crashed in the first quarter of 2018 it left many people depressed, but those who truly understood investing began to dollar-cost average and made tons of money in the next bull run when the coronavirus pandemic hit. Bitcoin's highest price in 2018 was about $17K, but rose to an all-time high of over $68K in November 2021; that's an increase of about 4x. While you cannot time the bottom or top of the market, money was made which is the whole point.

Say No

How can saying no help us to be pliable? Well, your inability to say no can ultimately ruin you. Sometimes you will have to say no to a supplier who is fixed in his approach, and switch to a new supplier who is working with the future in mind. Being pliable might call for some tough decisions along the way. We have to be able to say no and not feel bad about it, especially when we are sincere about our goals and what we want. We live in a world where everything is craving our attention. In his book *Give and Take*, Adam Grant says those who give too much at work lose focus on their own work. Their strength can be the very thing that causes their downfall. That, my friend, is what I mean when I tell you to say no sometimes.

Ego-Less Leadership

> *"A great man is always willing to be little."*
> - Ralph Waldo Emerson.

I believe there is a leader in everyone. Unfortunately, ego-less leadership is rare! Being pliable is a posture of humility overall and it works both ways, in the leader and the one being led. People in authority should be as equally humble as the people they are leading. This way we can maximize our potential.

The emerging leader's willingness to learn, to go see a guru, is an act of humility. Some may take the leader's humility for granted and that's okay, just be aware and set boundaries but don't give up because the right opportunity will come. Humility does not mean lie down for people to walk on you like a carpet. Know the difference between false and genuine humility.

Conversely, pride always precedes a fall. Pride will make you think you are the only one who is right, and when you continue with this attitude it will come to a point when people stop making suggestions because you don't listen. When you are not pliable, eventually you will pay a hefty price. Know that real life begins when we die to our ego and to self. There are so many materials available in this area, help yourself. I am only dropping a piece of wisdom here, hoping you will grab some. Will you make a conscious decision to be an ego-less follower or leader today?

FOUR
GUARD YOUR MIND

If you notice, our fingernails collect dirt naturally and it's up to us to clean them. Apply this metaphorically to our mind and it is clear – we need to guard it from taking on trash and becoming muddy. We must actively filter the information that enters our minds. Our brain works like an operating system; the way we guard our mind, determines the quality of its output. Garbage in—garbage out. Everything starts from this operating system; you are a genius! Look what we have done as humans. It is believed that the smartest among us are not utilizing 100% of their brain and even so, we have developed supercomputers and satellites that track people's current location. Now we're building flying hotels and space hotel ships. A group of engineers have even been able to make water out of thin air.

Just as we clean our nails, we need to guard our minds because we eventually become what we feed on. Mahatma Gandhi said, *"I will not let anyone walk through my mind with their dirty feet."* The reason is simple, the quality of your mind is dependent on you and nobody else. No one likes dirt, this is the reason car dealers will not sell a dirty car to you. Even when the car is a used car, they will detail it before presenting or handing it over to you. The same principle applies when we don't clean our minds, people will likely not buy from us until we get the dirt out.

Sometimes our nails are too dirty yet because we are so busy, we fail to pay attention. Then it takes someone to point out that our nails are not looking good. Dirty nails are not good for your health. Imagine using the same dirty nails to cook for others. Second, when our nails are too long and unkempt, they become sharp and we can unintentionally hurt others.

I understand we are all products of our environment. While this is true, we can make a choice either to run through the environment or let the environment run through us. You can either let your work, school etc. run through you or you can run through it.

Friedrich Nietzsche said in his book Beyond Good and Evil,
"In the end it must be as it is and always has been: great things remain for the great, abysses for the profound, nuances and shudders for the refined, and, in brief, all that is rare

for the rare. "This tells me there is greatness in this world, but it is reserved for the great, not because they are great but because they decided to be great. Let me say it in a different way – you are not poor until you die poor, meaning so long as there is life in you, things can change. You are not a dishonorable person until you die as one. You should in no way settle for less in life. Deep down within me I have always imagined a world of endless possibilities where there is no limit to the depths of our growth, but we need to make a conscious effort by guarding our minds. We can ascend to be the best versions of ourselves in intelligence, critical reasoning, parenting, strategic leadership, skill, influence, excellence and more. We can equally be gracious to others, if we choose to.

Perception

The first time I came across the phrase, "perception is reality," it lit up my world. A new fire was lit up on my inside, this even encouraged me to learn more about other cultures, other races and how they live. I cannot stress enough how much of a game changer it was for me. We see the world not as it is, but based on who we are. So, if there is one area I need you to focus so much energy on, it is in this area because it controls all the others. Life is all about perception! To go to the left or right is perception. To go through the narrow way or the broad way is perception. Poverty, wealth, abundance, scarcity, freedom all boils down to perception.

Freedom is not based on your location per se, you can be free in prison. Mike Tyson, the American former professional boxer, in a podcast said he had the best three years of his life in prison. The interviewer questioned why prison would be better than making millions boxing? Mike Tyson said, "*I had peace though.*" Making $30 million for one fight does not mean anything if you don't have peace, stability and balance. He went on to say your sanity is essential because it dictates every part of your life.

See, wearing a crown does not overturn how you perceive things. If you are someone who disrespects people, the crown won't change your behavior if that's just your perception. If your perception is darkened, a crown won't make it go away, you will have to expose it to light. That's the only way.

What separates the great from the small is perception. What separates the lion from the sheep is perception. Let me tell you a funny story about Samuel Hughes, a friend of mine. It is his perception that IT programmers are the best thing that ever happened to this world. He thinks programmers are the next best thing to God. He believes God is the best programmer of all time. I don't think we all have to be programmers, but I believe there is a program already operating inside us all. If we nurse it, and help it find expression, we can all become programmers in our own right. So maybe he was right after all, to a certain degree.

The real question is, are programmers relevant? Yes, but I wouldn't say they have the most important job of all. I believe we all have a part to play, and no matter how smart you are, or how important your role is, don't make others feel inferior around you. Rather always seek ways to empower people. By the time I am old, my heart desire is to see the younger generation go way beyond what we are able to achieve.

Growing up, I read another story in a John C. Maxwell book that shifted my mindset. The book told the story of a man whose only job was to sit in an office and think for the company. This guy made millions of dollars for the company. Isn't that brilliant? It stretched my perspective.

Equally compelling is a folk tale from India[4] that teaches intercultural awareness by illustrating how different perspectives lead to distinct points of view.

Long ago, six old men lived in a village in India. Each was born blind. The other villagers loved the old men and kept them away from harm. Since the men could not see the world for themselves, they had to imagine many of its wonders. They listened carefully to the stories told by travelers to learn what they could about life outside the village.

The men were curious about many of the stories they heard, but they were most curious about elephants. They were told that elephants could trample forests, carry huge burdens, and frighten young and old with their loud trumpet calls. But they also knew that the Rajah's daughter rode an elephant when she traveled in her father's kingdom. Would the Rajah let his daughter get near such a dangerous creature?

The old men argued day and night about elephants. "An elephant must be a powerful giant," claimed the first blind man. He had heard stories about elephants being used to clear forests and build roads.

"No, you must be wrong," argued the second blind man. "An elephant must be graceful and gentle if a princess is to ride on its back."

"You're wrong! I have heard that an elephant can pierce a man's heart with its terrible horn," said the third blind man.

"Please," said the fourth blind man. "You are all mistaken. An elephant is nothing more than a large sort of cow. You know how people exaggerate."

"I am sure that an elephant is something magical," said the fifth blind man. "That would explain why the Rajah's daughter can travel safely throughout the kingdom."

"I don't believe elephants exist at all," declared the sixth blind man. "I think we are the victims of a cruel joke."

Finally, the villagers grew tired of all the arguments, and they arranged for the curious men to visit the palace of the Rajah to learn the truth about elephants. A young boy from their village was selected to guide the blind men on their journey. The smallest man put his hand on the boy's shoulder. The second blind man put his hand on his friend's shoulder, and so on until all six men were ready to walk safely behind the boy who would lead them to the Rajah's magnificent palace.

When the blind men reached the palace, they were greeted by an old friend from their village who worked as a gardener on the palace grounds. Their friend led them to the courtyard. There stood an elephant. The blind men stepped forward to touch the creature that was the subject of so many arguments.

The first blind man reached out and touched the side of the huge animal. "An elephant is smooth and solid like a wall!" he declared. "It must be very powerful."

The second blind man put his hand on the elephant's limber trunk. "An elephant is like a giant snake," he announced.

The third blind man felt the elephant's pointed tusk. "I was right," he decided. "This creature is as sharp and deadly as a spear."

The fourth blind man touched one of the elephant's four legs. "What we have here," he said, "is an extremely large cow."

The fifth blind man felt the elephant's giant ear. "I believe an elephant is like a huge fan or maybe a magic carpet that can fly over mountains and treetops," he said.

The sixth blind man gave a tug on the elephant's coarse tail. "Why, this is nothing more than a piece of old rope. Dangerous, indeed," he scoffed.

The gardener led his friends to the shade of a tree. "Sit here and rest for the long journey home," he said. "I will bring you some water to drink."

While they waited, the six blind men talked about the elephant.

"An elephant is like a wall," said the first blind man. "Surely we can finally agree on that."

"A wall? An elephant is a giant snake!" answered the second blind man.

"It's a spear, I tell you," insisted the third blind man.

"I'm certain it's a giant cow," said the fourth blind man.

"Magic carpet. There's no doubt," said the fifth blind man.

"Don't you see?" pleaded the sixth blind man. "Someone used a rope to trick us."

Their argument continued and their shouts grew louder and louder.

"Wall!" "Snake!" "Spear!" "Cow!" "Carpet!" "Rope!"

"Stop shouting!" called a very angry voice.

It was the Rajah, awakened from his nap by the noisy argument.

"How can each of you be so certain you are right?" asked the ruler.

The six blind men considered the question. And then, knowing the Rajah to be a very wise man, they decided to say nothing at all.

"The elephant is a very large animal," said the Rajah kindly. "Each man touched only one part. Perhaps if you put the parts together, you will see the truth. Now, let me finish my nap in peace."

When their friend returned to the garden with the cool water, the six men rested quietly in the shade, thinking about the Rajah's advice.

"He is right," said the first blind man. "To learn the truth, we must put all the parts together. Let's discuss this on the journey home."

The first blind man put his hand on the shoulder of the young boy who would guide them home. The second blind man put a hand on his friend's shoulder, and so on until all six men were ready to travel together.

The moral of the folk tale is, as humans we tend to claim absolute truth based on our limited and subjective experiences. In so doing we ignore other people's limited, subjective experiences which may be equally true. You may have come across the 6/9 or M/W perspective. Each person is correct in their interpretation of the number or letter based on the position they are viewing it from.[4]

Status vs Substance Perspective

Don't think because someone is a celebrity it means they are more knowledgeable than you are. Having a huge following does not necessarily equate to being smarter. People have gifts that can mesmerize others but have no self-control or wisdom to guard their home. I wanted to add this so you have the right perspective about life. Being wealthy does give one an advantage to get some of the best counsellors or advisors available. Despite that, everyone can learn. Some people look good only because they have paid others to make them look good by giving them cookbooks and answers before coming on TV.

---

[4] John Godfrey Saxe, *The Blindmen and the Elephant*, (New York, NY, McGraw Hill, 1963)

So wake up, things and people are not always as they appear.

How You Treat People – Perspective

How you deal with people is nearly the mirror-image of who you truly are, it reflects your values. With maturity comes patience and authority over circumstances and issues. Being able to master your soul is a rare commodity which gives you the upper hand to dominate your world. Many times you can easily distinguish a good listener from a bad listener by their body posture, level of detail and attentiveness.

Organizational Iceberg - Perspective

To guard your mind does not mean you put on a physical helmet. It is a helmet that cannot be seen by the naked eye, nevertheless, it is a helmet that needs to be worn at all times.

Are you familiar with the concept of an organizational iceberg? What sinks a ship is usually not seen. Why? Because it lies below sea level. Many factors can contribute to sinking a ship. It could be rocks or anything hidden under the surface of the water, so seeing just the surface does you no good, you must look beneath.

When it comes to our bodies, the things that matter most cannot be seen, yet they are what keep us alive. The heart, liver, kidneys, and other internal organs are hidden, but take one of them out and your life may drastically change. Often times we focus on trivial external things, spending so much time feeding the outward which profits little. Guarding your mind implies taking a holistic viewpoint to take stock of your life. It surprises me how we spend hundreds of thousands of dollars buying cars, but when we are asked to pay even half of that to sustain our health we cry. We would rather spend money on pleasure, but we need our health to enjoy these fleeting pleasures.

Exercising Our Minds

Another way to guard our mind is to exercise it. Groom it to the point where it becomes automatic, knowing when to reject or accept information. It needs to get to a point where you don't even have to think twice about what is good or bad anymore. There is a scripture that connects to this thought. It's in Hebrews 5:14 (ASV) and states, *"But solid food is for full-grown men, even those who by reason of use have their senses exercised to discern good and evil."*

When we exercise our minds to a certain level, they start to work within strong tested boundaries where we can be consistent with our thoughts and actions. We can achieve this when we program our minds to think positively. As politician and motivational speaker Les Brown says, *"Only quality people (OQP) are allowed in here."* This will help you to walk, stay, and execute in the light.

Rain can destroy, but it is good overall. As you desire the rain to fall, someone else desires the sun – that my friend is the beauty of life. Be wise enough to embrace both worlds, as what favors you might not favor another person. Adaptability is key to engaging the various seasons of life.

FIVE
INTERDEPENDENCE

I want you to look at the placement of your nail; it rests on a nail bed that I call a motherboard. Throughout your life, the motherboard does not move, the nail sits on it. For some people, figuratively, the motherboard might be your support system – family, father or mother figures, mentors, close allies, etc. This is a great reminder never to forget your roots, irrespective of whether you had everything you wanted or not. If nothing at all, your roots gave you a start at life.

Also, there is no such thing as a self-made man in my world. I understand the hustle, but a closer look at your success in hindsight will unveil key players (the good, the bad, and the ugly) who made it possible for you to be where you are. So, before you think you achieved everything all by yourself, pause and rethink! Reflect on your childhood days, perhaps you would be dead by now if someone did not take the knife from your hands or save you from falling down the stairs.

Personally, I believe there is a time of separation in every man's life where you have to begin to dig your own well. Some call it the oven room, a place where you get to decide what you really want out of this life. It does not cancel the fact we still need people to survive. No man is an island and to be honest, it is not good for a man to be alone. For some people it might take your spouse traveling away from home with the kids for this reality to kick in.

A call for interdependence also means, no one has everything, and nobody has nothing. No matter how hard I try, I can never be you and you can't be me. That is how the world is programmed, so we have to learn and interdepend on each another. In another dimension, we are somewhat separated into talents, skills, and areas of expertise. When we need entertainment, there are people built for that. When our cars break down, we know where to go.

No matter how bad a situation is, it can improve; and no matter how good a situation is, it can also be improved. However, to achieve this we need people. Independence is not necessarily a blessing; dependence could be a curse and annoying to some degree at times. Interdependence then is golden.

It's no wonder Stephen R. Covey in his book *The 7 Habits of Highly Effective People* said, "*Interdependence is a higher value than independence*". In plain words I say, the power of synergy is greater than the power of one.

Many philosophers have broken life into three phases.

> ➢ PHASE 1 - DEPENDENCE: Where parents take care of you, this will not last forever.

> ➢ PHASE 2 - INDEPENDENCE: Where you move out to rent or own your own house, you begin to pay bills, buy your own food, clothes, etc.

> ➢ PHASE 3 - INTERDEPENDENCE: Real maturity is interdepending on each other. This is not to say you are immature if you don't marry, but we will use marriage for the sake of illustration. The moment you decide to marry, in the ideal setting, both sides of the family need to agree before the marriage takes place. In marriage, spouses agree before making certain decisions.

Better still, take a house for example. The beauty of any house is not seen in the individual brick, but one brick interdependent on another. Huge towers look good for this same reason. Institutions and nations rise and become powerful adhering to this truth. In an interdependent relationship, no one is superior or inferior. The best way to approach this ideology is to have a servant leader mindset.

Can you type with only one finger? Absolutely. Can you type with two fingers from each side? Yes. But typing with one finger from just one hand is much slower than one from both hands. Then compare it to when you have all 10 fingers on the keyboard. The effectiveness is indisputable. Such is life!

SIX
PROTECTOR

Nails serve as a protective covering. Although small, they still have the potential to serve as a shield from sharp objects. I want you to pause for a second, imagine living in a world with no protection. Having emails without passwords, cars or houses without locks, or your favorite wine without a cork. Would you honestly be comfortable living in such a world? The obvious answer is "no". You may not know about keratin, but nails are made of it. Keratin is a type of extremely tough protein that forms the cells that make up tissue for our nails and other parts of the body (including the outer layer of skin). Animal's hooves, horns, and teeth are also made up of keratin. They are akin to claws in other animals. Keratin plays an important role in nail heath, and protects our nails from damage by making them strong and resilient.

When you think about keratin in nails being a protector, what comes to your mind? For me it is insurance. Insurance is the most common example of risk financing. Risk financing is a form of protection used to cover losses or pay for losses. If I were you, I would take the following forms of insurance seriously going forward.

> ➢ HEALTH INSURANCE: This is a form of protection that helps pay medical expenses. As humans, sicknesses or communicable outbreaks are inevitable. We didn't call for a pandemic, but it came. This is not the first time the world has suffered through, or recovered from, a pandemic and there is no telling what the future might hold. We have experienced the Spanish Flu, SARS and Ebola, just to name a few. Anytime this happens, people with underlying health issues suffer the most. For such people this also means high medical bills. Not having "keratin" in the form of insurance will result in massive medical bills, or hell, for you.

> ➢ DISABILITY INSURANCE: This helps to cover any losses you incur from a serious injury. It also replaces your salary while you are unable to work, allowing you to meet your basic needs.

> ➢ LIFE INSURANCE: Helps to pay expenses and provide income for your spouse and children in case of premature death or death.

I am certified by The Institutes in "Insurance Essentials", so let me give you a brief history about insurance in the United States.

The concept of insurance began in Europe and spread across several countries they colonized. Insurance in the United States evolved from the insurance practices of the British. During the early days in the States, fire companies leveraged on fire marks. Fire marks were metal plates (see examples pictured above) used to identify buildings covered by a fire insurance company. In other words, the first private fire departments needed a way to identify which buildings were covered by their respective company. Each fire company developed its own fire mark which was placed on insured buildings. When a fire occurred, all fire companies responded to the building and the company associated with the corresponding fire mark on the building would fight the fire; no others would get involved. This approach to handling fires was found to be ineffective and after ten years gave way to public fire departments that responded to all fires.

To buttress my other point, why would you insure your car, properties, and company finances but not insure your life? Putting this in context, when we buy package policies from insurance companies what we are doing is seeking some sort of protection or 'keratin'. To bring the point home, what is your keratin? What protects you from damage? The answers might differ. Whatever the case may be, make sure you stay connected to whomever, or whatever, is your source. For some people, keratins are the support system who watch our back. For others it might mean your family of believers who keep you in prayer. Why would you unplug from what gives you life?

SEVEN
START SMALL

The young shall grow! When we compare the nails of toddlers to adults, we see a big difference with respect to size – so don't be afraid to start small. History is replete with people who started small, and look where some of them are today. Figure 1 is a popular picture which shows the humble beginnings of some of today's major companies.

Figure 1

Great things often start small. In a CNBC article on Richard Branson published in 2018[5], Richard Branson relays he is proof that very little money is needed to start a business. Actually, he had no money to put toward the business when he started. Virgin is just one of many examples which highlight some of the companies we know and love started tiny. In the article, Branson noted he receives many pitches from upcoming entrepreneurs which have a common line: "I need x amount to get started." According to Branson, this sort of mindset or thinking is a mistake. Start with what you have!

Remember motivational speaker Zig Ziglar said, *"You don't have to be great to start, but you have to start to be great."* Greatness is encoded in the process. Don't chase money. Follow your dream and money will chase you. Conversely, waiting to get all the money before you start is a bad idea. Ideas themselves are like magnets – they will attract the right people and the right resources according to the laws of nature.

---

[5] CNBC, Richard Branson funded his first business at 16 for less than $2,000, 28 Aug 2018, (www.cnbc.com/2018/08/28/richard-branson-launched-his-first-business-for-less-than-2000.html).

What matters is you defeat your mind, kill self-doubt, and start with what you can afford today (this includes angel investors and whatever is within your means)

Source: Successpictures

Obstacles to Starting

If you lose track of your objective, you will only see obstacles. However, if the only thing you see is the objective, then the obstacle must give way. What most people have not been taught is this truth – the more challenging your life is, the greater potential it has to inspire others.

This sort of ideology usually puts faith over fear. Many people say, "I really wish I had the right connection, if only I had _____ and _____ then this would happen." Wrong, the key is to get started. Canadian self-help author Bob Proctor encourages entrepreneurs by saying, *"Faith and fear both demand you believe in something you cannot see. You choose!"* So why choose fear? Feed your faith and starve your fears.

Here is a life hack, always opt for the harder option or route, not the path of least resistance. The moment you are able to do something significant it puts you on the world stage, while choosing the easier route could increase the time it takes for you to reach your goal. Everybody wants to connect with champions and people who are fixing problems.

Fear

Many have defined FEAR as "False Evidence Appearing Real," but to me the word FEAR stands for "For Every Average Rockstar". Although we are born rockstars, speaking metaphorically, many will die as average. Somewhere along the way many will get trapped in safe zones, believing they are minding their own business. Being afraid of the opinion of others cripples. The painful truth about fear is this – fear does not stop death, it stops life.

I was watching a television series called *Prison Break*; in it I learned something I will never forget. In a conversation between the characters Michael and Sarah, Michael said something like, "When they tell you not to open a door, the day you open it you realize there is another door behind that door. Open it, and you will find another one and you realize there are several, perhaps 100s or 1000s, of them." It is literally endless. Your ability to unlock, or go through, those gates is what makes the difference. Such is life, every door we dare to open becomes the steppingstone for the next door.

Sometimes it is not just fear, but pain. Like writer Robin Sharma says, "*Pain is potential unexpressed.*" If you know doing xyz is what will take you there, then do it. Fear is a useful emotion all the same. It can save you from many troubles. But fear has adverse effects too because fear cuts deeper than swords.

The good thing is, fear is in the eye of the beholder - so don't let it be in you. Once I read quote from a friend of mine, artist Nii Abbey, which said, "*You will never know how good a perfume smells until you apply pressure on its head.*" Perhaps that's exactly what you have been running from, but after reading this I hope you finally make that jump and apply that pressure. Take that leap of faith and I'll see you at the top!

Fear is just a bunch of emotions that come together anytime you try to leave the safe house or your comfort zone. The world says fear is bad but I believe fear is only an opportunity for bravery training. The beauty about life and living can be summed up in this quote:

"In the midst of winter, I found there was, within me, an invincible summer. And that makes me happy. For it says that no matter how hard the world pushes against me, within me, there's something stronger – something better, pushing right back."
- Albert Camus

Another way I define fear is ironically - "For Every Amazing/Awesome/Astounding Rockstar". This is only for those who are able to defeat fear and make that jump. So don't let fear stop you. Remember fear doesn't stop death, it stops life.

Identity Crisis

One obstacle that prevents people from starting is an identity crisis. "Cogito, ergo sum," translated into English as "I think, therefore I am" is a Latin philosophical proposition by René. Would you agree that it would be an error to see a member of British royalty homeless and begging for alms on the street? That would be a surprise, correct? In the same vein, don't think yourself less just because you were not born into the royal family. That's why I quoted "I think, therefore I am." I came upon this quote when I visited Bill Gates at the Gates Foundation some time ago and it resonated in my mind - *"All lives have equal value."*

I am a firm believer that all lives intrinsically have equal value. So, say to yourself - "I am ROYALTY". Having this mentality as you sojourn through life can significantly improve the quality of your life. How you ask? Identity is a driver. Knowing your self-worth and having a sense of innate royalty drives self-confidence. I would choose someone who is self-confident over someone who is not, because insecurity can breed a toxic environment in a workplace.

An insecure person may consider eliminating others to stand out and feel intimidated in the presence of highly skilled people. On the other hand, when people belong to royal stock, even if it only exists in their mind, when they finally get to the palace, they don't feel that it is an accomplishment. Rather, they feel it is their "rightful" place. They imagine that way because they already think of themselves as royals, this is what motivates people to start believing in who they are. It's having the confidence that "if they can do it, so can I." It is not pride if this thought is born from a sincere heart.

Your dream should not become your demise because you have an identity crisis. Identity dictates our different routes and destinations in life, where we go and where we do not go, our dos and don'ts are all tied to our identity. Where will you likely find a gambler, in the casino, correct? Because that's what he loves doing. Note, I didn't say that's "who he is", because he can stop this habit if he decides. But until then, this will be his identity and his identity will dictate where to find him. Where will you find a nurse? A hospital or clinic. You will not find nurses dressed in their work attire or uniforms in the club.

Identity is a Master Driver

It is imperative for you to know who you are. When the identity crisis is settled, it eliminates a lot of clutter and gives you clarity because your actions will always align with your identity. In other words, identity dictates behavior.

I kid you not, if you truly believe in something, your behavior will align with it. Identity always comes before behavior. We have a mental image, a portrait of how we see ourselves and the world. If you have the right image, your life will turn out right, all other things being equal, and the converse is true. The outcomes of life are dependent on our most dominant picture.

There is an illustration I came across some time ago. If you tell a three-year-old girl to walk across the stage, she will care less about what others think. Give the same command to a 30-year-old woman and the outcome will be totally different. She will walk across the stage, but you will notice the way she carries herself is different. Almost like her walk is calculated, there is a way she swings her hands, especially if she has great nails. What's the difference? The older woman recognizes something the younger one does not – she has an identity. Obviously, that explains why kings and presidents talk in a way which contrasts to how commoners and those not in authority talk.

When Christopher Columbus was looking for sailors in preparation for his first voyage west, he allegedly posted this:

WANTED

Bold, brave, adventurous souls to accompany me on an exciting voyage.

Final destination? HOME.

First few stops? Uncertain, but probably off the maps and charts.

Length of journey? Unknown.

Hazards and dangers? Many.

Cost to you? Your time, money and maybe your life itself.

Rewards? God alone knows, but God alone decides.

Opportunity? The one of a lifetime!

~Christopher Columbus, 1491

The journey might have been far in his case, the length was even unknown, but he knew he had to start from somewhere and that somewhere was not his "home". He needed to start small in order to finish great. Like they say, a thousand-mile journey begins with a step. Small drops of water make a mighty ocean and that's how Christopher Columbus set out to discover America supposedly.

Final Destination

In Christopher Columbus' advertisement, the final destination was defined as home. Home to some people is their "actualization hallmark," but keep in mind, success is never final! The end is buried in your first step, that's why I encourage you to start. If you don't start, you will never finish. Realizing this truth earlier in life will expedite the manifestation of your destiny and greatness. The manifestation of greatness is not instant, it unfolds one heartbeat at a time as we improve and progress. When you set out, it often looks like you will never get there. Reading this book right now might be changing your world, one word and one heartbeat at a time. As I paraphrase a few lines of Steven Curtis Chapman's song *One Heartbeat at a Time* you'll get my point - making history with every touch and every smile, you may not see it now, but I believe that time will tell how you are changing your world.

First Few Stops? Uncertain

Every giant dream starts with a degree of uncertainty, then as you continue to think on it, it expands and grows into other branches, but all the dreams come from one root. Who would have thought that Richard Branson started with magazines and today owns airlines? Who would have thought Samsung started by selling noodles, yes you read that right. Some of these stories blow my mind when I contrast where they started with where they are today. Samsung was founded as a grocery trading store on March 1, 1938, by Lee Byung-Chull in Korea. He started by selling noodles and other goods that were being exported to China and its provinces after production.

Length of Journey

The length of the journey is unknown. We live in the unknown every day. That is why we say no one knows tomorrow. If some people knew buying their dream car was what would kill them, perhaps they wouldn't buy it. The point here in reference to this chapter is sometimes we may miss our deadlines and that is okay. We may not get everything right, and that is okay. I would choose a quality release over a rushed half-baked product or software that is released in the market too soon.

You can become so focused on crossing the finish line that without even realizing it you have. That's because there is no finish line in your mind. Where you will be will forever remain a mystery. For many, the joy comes in just knowing how far they have come. The length of a marriage might be unknown. No one marries their enemy, yet not all marriages make it to the end. Even if you get to the end, the chances of both of you dying the same day is rare. The same applies to companies and other enterprises. So, take time to celebrate the small wins as well as the big wins. Be grateful in life, because the length of the journey is unknown.

Hazards and Dangers? Many

Start small, let the naysayers mock you. Today we can learn from great people in history like Michael Jordan, Disney, and Oprah. I am sure there are tons of stories you know too about how far they have come.

Keep in mind there could be potential dangers. One of them is envy. Honey is sweet and because it is sweet it attracts a lot of bees. Therefore, be aware of the bees, but do not let them deter you. Let people say and do their worst but keep moving. If you are ever going to get to the top, you had better grow a thick skin now.

Cost to You

Your cost is your time, your energy, your talents, your (and possibly other's) money and maybe your life itself.

Time Factor

Time is precious, it is the currency of life so trade it wisely. You cannot afford to sleep your life away. Alarms are good for reminders, but if that's the only thing that wakes you up then you haven't started dreaming yet. There comes a time where your responsibilities alone could be so enormous that it keeps you awake. When your conscience is tied to the lives of millions or billions, how do you sleep? Any mistake you make can be costly.

There are many outstanding things about time. One in particular that strikes me is no one can stop time regardless of their money, power or fame. Time is no respecter of wealth or status; it serves us all the same. We say nothing in life is fair, but I believe time plays a fair game and if time was a president, it would definitely earn my vote.

"You can buy a clock, but you cannot buy time."
- Matshona Dhliwayo

Even as you read this book the clock is ticking, whether you are conscious of it or not. I think everyone should be "time literate," it is very important. Let me tell you a story. I had a dialogue with this lady some years ago. From her responses, I easily discovered she wasn't time literate. So, I pitched an idea that would open her mind to the awesomeness and dreadfulness of time altogether. I said to her, "do you realize you are drawing nearer to your grave right now as we speak?" She looked at me in shock. I continued, pointing out that she could get more money, but not more time. At this point, I had her attention. My only intention was to help her put her life in order. Thankfully she was the teachable type, so it wasn't difficult to encourage her to start small now with the big picture in mind!

Money Factor

Money answers all things! While true, it's not the entire truth because wisdom says otherwise. I say that money answers most things, but not all things because there are some things money just cannot buy. You cannot buy life, safety, or security among others. Great leaders, with great wealth, have been assassinated time and time again. When it comes to money, whoever loves money never has enough.

In a book entitled, *What Are You Living For?: Investing Your Life in What Matters Most* by Pat Williams, he had this to say about money - *"Money can buy a house, but not a home; a bed, but not rest; food, but not an appetite; medicine, but not health; information, but not wisdom; thrills, but not joy; associates, but not friends; servants, but not loyalty; flattery, but not respect."*

Similarly, money can buy you a computer, but not brains; finery, but not beauty; luxuries, but not culture; amusement, but not happiness; and obedience, but not faithfulness. According to singer-songwriter Garth Brooks, *"You are not wealthy until you have something money can't buy."*

Getting back to the point, starting small doesn't mean do it on your own. Starting small may require raising capital for your startup and there are so many ways of financing. You can start with family and friends depending on the amount or try angel investors, ICOs, etc.

Life

Life equals blood, sweat and tears. Find your niche and commit to it. Times of discomfort means "pay attention here." Commit to your work, fall in love with it, and go to work. They say life is short, but if it is well lived it can be long enough.

Rewards? God Alone Knows

Many great musicians and highly skilled people have confessed over the years that after they have put in all the hard work, the results are really dependent on a higher force. Their perceived hit songs sometimes don't cut it, while the least expected one sometimes becomes the hit. It is definitely not a one size fits all but there is an atom of truth here. It is only wise for us to sow seeds and sow as many as we can with the best of our abilities in each of them. There is a way you can leave your stamp on your work, so when people walk into a place they can tell you were there. I hope that can be said about you.

Opportunity? The Once in a Lifetime!

Although it is risky to the point where it can cost our lives; although there will be stops, potential hazards and dangers; although the length of the journey may be unknown; we cannot give up, especially when the opportunity of a lifetime opens up. This is the reason some will pay over $200k on something, or spend millions to go the moon, and others won't understand. We have different priorities. As much as you want to help others, don't let their poverty mindset and opinions scare away your dream of a lifetime.

It is said poor people know the price of everything and the value of nothing. Rich people on the other hand, know the value of everything and the price of nothing. Let me add a qualifier here - "some" poor people and "some" rich people - because I believe this quote is defective without allowing exceptions, while the phrase "rich people" is subjective. In light of that, let me remind you again - we only have one life to live, the clock is ticking, and we don't have time!

Nabeel Qureshi, a Pakistani-American author and apologist, spoke these words after being diagnosed with stage IV stomach cancer, "we don't have time." Imagine if you were told you only have two months to live? How would you live your life? What would you do differently? This was an eye opener for me. We really don't have time. It is lack of revelation that makes us think we have all the time in the world, so we sleep. What is your life mission?

EIGHT
PARALLEL LANES

Let's do a simple exercise, place your hands on a flat surface like a desk or a table. What do you observe? Do you see that each of your fingernails have their own lanes? There could be a few cases of deformity where one finger will cross the other. But really, the human nails are carved in their own lane, it's a dedicated parallel lane.

When you see people crossing lanes into other people's lives, it is most likely because they are struggling with an identity crisis. There are exceptions to this conventional rule of thumb. There are times when people of great destiny will meet along the way. Their meeting does not constitute crossing lanes. Although we are in parallel lanes, there may be a time your car breaks down and you need help. This is what can be referred to as destiny helpers. This type of help demonstrates love which is a commonality that binds the human race together.

The Asante people of Ghana in West Africa have a local proverb, "nsa teaa nyinaa nyɛ pɛ". It implies all fingers do not have the same height. So stay in your own lane because "Me nya wo ayɛ, yɛ musuo" (wishing to be someone else is an abomination). They say that because you never know what the person you are wishing to be like is also going through. Staying in your lane can mean so many things. It can mean - do things based on your level. Perhaps there is a time in life where you can afford to buy 10 houses at one time with no hassle. Alternatively, there is a time when even one is a challenge. The point is to build your starter home based on your level. Marry at your level; there are some men and women who are "high maintenance." This can be a red flag which may lead to countless arguments, so stay in your lane.

I used to envy people with great height but then I looked at how some of them suffer to bend before they enter cars, or to enter doors in homes. They constantly have to be aware of their surroundings to avoid getting hurt by a low doorway or low hanging ceiling fan. Realizing this, I must agree with the Akan proverb that says to love yourself and not wish to be somebody else.

We don't all have the same weight, body mass index, status, stature etc. Some are tall, some are short but that does not necessarily translate to the capacity of a man. I say it this way, the short man is designed to do something that

84

the giant cannot do; the giant also has an advantage over the short man, so it is only wise they pair together.

Different Types of 'Parallel' Lanes in Life

I intentionally used parallel lanes because no matter what you are doing, there are people who have gone ahead of you. You will not be the first musician or sportsman to walk on this earth. Even though we have different gifts and talents, we are somewhat batched in our respective parallel lanes.

Some of these lanes include, but are not limited to:

Wise Lane

This lane is for my movers and shakers. This is when you are doing the right thing and you know it without a shred of doubt. These are tested and true lanes, the ancient path. There are times in our lives that we have done the right things, but did not even realize how good it was until the results proved it. There are some things you may be doing in your life (i.e. having a family and marriage) that are right, but you don't know it is really the right thing until you attend a marriage conference and hear similar stories that complement yours. I have a personal conviction that those who strive for mastery would one day come to a place of utter consciousness where they know for sure that what they're doing is the right thing. That is where you've got to be, my friend, in the wise lane.

If you have a lot of friends in the wise lane circus, try to work with them as much as you can. Now, let's play a fun game, we will match each lane to a phone call. In terms of a phone call, the wise lane will be a received, or an answered, call. Don't miss the call to be on the wise lane. There are friends who will inspire and challenge you to study in school or to stick it out in your calling, these all fall in the wise lane.

Life Lane

This lane has people who are full of energy, cheerleaders, people who are willing to give it a shot, willing to try new things, and excited about new opportunities. I highly recommend this lane. In a circle of friends on this lane, it will not be long before you catch up because birds of a feather, flock together. In terms of a phone call, this would be an answered call.

Death Lane

Have you ever met someone whose words were always gloomy? They always think the world is coming to an end. Get out of that lane before they kill you. In terms of a phone call, this would be a blocked call. You only pick up such calls to listen or if you intend to speak life into their situation, but never for advice.

Dumb Lane

This lane is for those who are not abreast of matters going on in the world and will not bother to find out. They grab and eat everything that looks good to the eyes. For example, a prudent man will tell you we do not live to eat, rather we eat to live. In essence, you cannot spend your whole life on food. You also don't eat every junk food out there. A man with a vision in life watches everything he takes, be it spiritual or physical food. In terms of a phone call, this will be a missed call. Only pick up, or pay attention to, friends in this lane when you see from their actions they are ready to grow. If you are in this lane, get out or else you'll waste valuable time.

Peace Lane

Do you know someone who always seeks peace? They will do everything they can to settle a dispute or make sure it ends well for everyone. The problem in this lane is attempting to please everyone, especially in this era of political correctness. You must stand up for what you believe in, let people know who you are and the values you represent. In terms of a phone call, this is an answered call, with caution and tactfulness.

Happiness Lane

The problem in the happiness lane is that happiness is fleeting, and it is provisional. Although not limited to enjoyment or events, it is largely based on occasions and situations. However, do enjoy things as they come along. Take time to make memories and enjoy the ceremonies as they come. People in this lane are usually happy-go-lucky. They just want to have fun. Answer this call if you have the bandwidth because it cannot always be fun time, there must be a balance.

Joy Lane

Joy is rarely used these days, but it does not mean that joy is extinct. Many who find joy usually have a deep sense of spiritual connection. Whatever gives you joy, I recommend you to not discard it, for joy is a great virtue. Joy, unlike happiness, is not fleeting. This is an inner witness that is steadfast and sure. This should be an answered call.

Mind Your Business Lane

Don't get distracted if someone is going to a different destination. Focus on yours. If they need help, offer to help if you can, but mind your business. There is no point in being jealous or worried about what others are doing. If you know you are in the right lane, it is okay to pat others on the back. Celebrate people until it is your turn. When it is your turn, continue to celebrate others and allow others to celebrate with you. Give credit where it is due. There is enough space for everybody. In terms of a phone call this would be a "do not disturb."

NINE
BE SENSITIVE (DISCERN)

We grew up using a blade to cut our fingernails and I remember there were times I had to be extremely careful or else I would end up cutting myself. At times, cutting my nails wasn't fun, it made me feel weak and the nails themselves were sensitive. Can you relate to this?

Here is a bonus health tip not directly related to sensitivity. Some people feel pain after cutting their nails and one reason could be a nail infection or injury. It may be helpful to take your own clippers and other nail tools to the salon to avoid exposure to bacteria or fungus carried on other's nails.

Back to the point, not being sensitive is how some kings have lost their thrones. Some presidents lost an election because they were insensitive in their speeches and actions. Some wives and husbands have lost their relationship; and some leaders have lost their positions due to this same reason.

Once I had the chance to lead a group of people in marriage counselling. Thankfully, I was sensitive enough when we touched on couples who had lost a child. Little did I know the counsellor and his wife had been there before, and he shared some of the insensitive things people said to them about the loss of their child. Some went to the extent of saying it is okay because they still had three more kids. While this was true, it was not okay and to say that is a no no! It simply shows how insensitive some people can be. When you are talking about touchy subjects in a group setting, be sure to approach them tactfully. It doesn't mean we have to be overly politically correct the way our society has become, but there is always a wise way to handle situations.

Empathy

You should not feel apathy or unmoved by war in a distant land because either we are all home, or no one is. The next time it might be your land and that's why being sensitive is the basis of empathy. We cheer with those who cheer, and we mourn with those who mourn. We are all sensitive in different ways and degrees.

In a TEDx talk given by Elena Herdieckerhoff entitled *The Gentle Power of Highly Sensitive People*[6] she spoke of highly sensitive people (HSP). Some of the people who have blessed our world have been HSP. Arguably not all HSP are heroes, but we cannot discount the likes of Mother Teresa, Mahatma Gandhi, Mozart and Leonardo da Vinci who was known to be a polymath, and Anaïs Nin, a French-born American diarist, essayist, novelist, and writer of short stories and erotica. These HSPs used their highly sensitive nature to heal the world because they could feel the pain of others. Gandhi is believed to have had long fasts that went on for years without a square meal for political causes, for freedom, and for justice to prevail.

---

[6] Elena Herdieckerhoff, The Gentle Power of Highly Sensitive People, TEDx, 21 May 2016 (www.youtube.com/@TEDx).

TEN
BLEED

Occasionally we cut skin when we attempt to cut our fingernails. There are seasons like that when all the odds are against us. One of the painful things we all go through in life is when we lose a loved one or some unfortunate incident happens. We ask questions that we have no answers to. During such moments it is okay to cry or bleed, but after a while you will have to pick yourself up and find strength to continue the journey. Most importantly, it keeps us in check and keeps us humble knowing we are no different from the one who just passed on. Many times loss also serves as a booster to put our house in order and to do the best we can before our time comes.

Bleeding is essential, it gives us a free reality check. Suddenly, we become conscious of things of which we may have lost sight. Have you bled lately? What caused it? Was there anything to learn from it? There are so many lessons to learn from bleeding, it causes us to be mindful of our surroundings and ourselves.

People react to bleeding differently. Some smile while they are bleeding and others just can't. I recall washing my face once and I accidentally cut myself somewhere around my nose area because I had long fingernails. Today, I am careful when washing my face and I remind myself to keep my nails short. I bled for a while, then put salt water on it to stop the bleeding. I share this story to say I have had personal experience and learned my lesson from it.

One of the ways we can heal after a painful experience is to listen to songs that are therapeutic. Good music is refreshing to the soul and that is one of the things I would recommend. So, take some time out to heal but don't stay down for too long. Having friends who can empathize with your bleeding and offer a shoulder to lean on and find comfort are also ways to heal. The right choice of words can help stabilize and give life to someone who is downcast.

Positive Bleeding

You may wonder if there are any benefits to bleeding. Have you ever donated blood? Would you consider donating again? You never know who you might be saving especially if you are type O negative, a universal donor. Donating blood is a form of bleeding, one that doesn't come with too much pain, but the process of blood coming out is what I refer to as bleeding. All the same, I consider this a positive form of bleeding and the benefits far outweigh the momentary pain or discomfort. The discomfort of losing blood varies, it could lead to dizziness and tiredness in the case of excessive blood loss. In spite of this, together let's help hospitals save lives or even the lives of loved ones around us. Another upside with this type of bleeding is our bodies are able to generate new blood.

Negative Effects to Bleeding

Negatively, some bleeding can leave emotional and physical scars. Scars of the heart can linger on for years and if we don't take care, they can affect us negatively in so many ways. For example, sometimes people experiencing a broken heart don't heal completely before they enter into new relationships. It's not fair that another man or woman be liable or expected to pay for someone else's mistakes, but it happens all the time. Be open to your new partner, share your story, and be sure you are in a good place before you let another person into your space. Scars are usually not beautiful, but if someone is unwilling to accept you and your scars, they are probably not worth hanging around in the first place.

There is an African proverb that says, *"One who loves you, loves you with your dirt."* Dirt here refers to your past and scars. True love covers a plethora of sins, and to forgive is divine.

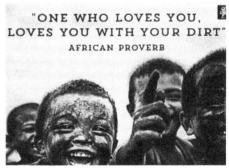

"ONE WHO LOVES YOU, LOVES YOU WITH YOUR DIRT"
AFRICAN PROVERB

Source: African Proverb

We are humans and scars are part of life. It's really tough and rare to go through life without scars. It does not work like that. To live without scars makes you a walking dead. People who expect to have everything smooth and easy don't have the right outlook on life. Our heart is always beating, the rate goes up and down. When you are in the summer of life be humble, because the winter train is soon going to come for you. Enjoy every moment in and out of season for this is our lot in life.

Not expecting any downward trends or things to never go wrong in life is not being practical. It is not realistic and that is living a life of fantasy. Even in your home there are times things will spoil. You may have to fix a roof leak, change a broken water heater or AC unit, etc.

The stock market and investing are something else that can make you bleed. Some time ago, I listened to a hedge fund manager talk about losing approximately $3 billion because the market tanked. One can only imagine managing the portfolios of so many people and having so many lives depend on you. What did he do? Being a seasoned investor, he was smart enough to HODL ("hold on for dear life") through the downturn and in time he recovered all the money back with profit. Panic selling is never a good idea; the stock market, as they say, is a tool for transferring money from the impatient to the patient. Wealth is patient, I hope you learn something here or else you are going to bleed and regret your decisions thereafter.

To sum it up, all our scars tell a story. These scars could be physical or physiological (mental). Make them count.

ELEVEN
BEGIN AND END

Fingernails and toenails begin to form inside the womb at week 11 of pregnancy with the nails themselves beginning to grow at week 12. Nails do have a begin and end date. Flowers wither and die, such is life. All shall pass away so make hay while the sun shines.

To recap some of the lessons learned from earlier chapters; true change and transformation begins from the inside. The foundation has to be strong enough to survive the storms that come with life, so you don't go back to the way things were before. Birth and death also teach us that life is a process. Great things take time to build. Rome was not built in a day, so do not rush the process. When considering the trajectory of the beginning and ending dates, it is the dash between the dates that matters most. The dash represents the life of the individual or a thing. There are many quotes that have been written about life. Far too many to place here, but there are a few that matter to me.

"In the end, it's not the years in your life that count.
It's the life in your years."
- Abraham Lincoln

"If life were predictable it would cease to be life,
and be without flavor."
- Eleanor Roosevelt

"Life is a succession of lessons which
must be lived to be understood."
- Ralph Waldo Emerson & Helen Keller

"He blossoms for a moment like a flower—and withers;
as the shadow of a passing cloud, he quickly disappears."
- Job 14:2 (TLB)

"Life is like a candle in the wind."
- Elton John

"May you live all the days of your life."
- Jonathan Swift

Growing Up

As we grow up our parents act as our geofence. A geofence is a virtual geographic boundary, defined by GPS or RFID technology. It enables software to trigger a response when a mobile device enters or leaves a particular area. A range is set (i.e. 200m/656ft safe zone) and it can identify when a child has departed from, or arrived in, a specific location such as school or home.

Parents were there to hold us when we cried. It seemed at times they would appear out of nowhere almost like magic, especially if you were the last born. I remember being the last born for a while and enjoying all the treats and being spoon-fed. I did not like it then when my mother gave birth to another child after me. It felt like this other person was going to take my sweet spot. Many will deny it, but those of us who have younger siblings have all been there before. That meant all my rights and privileges were going to be stripped away and now all the attention was suddenly on the new baby.

Karma

Beware of karma; for a man reaps whatever he sows. If you sow grape seeds you shouldn't expect to reap oranges.

Life as a Race

We have to hurry to give the baton to the next generation. They might not be in view, but their ability to go further and possibly win is largely dependent on us.

Commitment

Commitment is key to winning in this race called life. Find your niche and commit to it. Become the expert and dominate in your area of expertise.

Reinvent Yourself (Rebirth)

You will go through a series of rebirths or reinventions if you allow it to happen. In your life, there will come a time where you have to drastically reinvent yourself, your methods, your approach to things, and your communication style to suit a given type of audience or situation. This is not something you do lightly or haphazardly. This is for those who wish to evolve

94

and desire to lead effectively. Things may be working, and you may be productive but real effectiveness says you can do more, you can do better. Bear in mind, your reinvention is not done in order to be seen by others, this is not for show. It is for you to stay relevant in the community.

Awareness – Reality Check

After reading this book one of my desires is that you, like nails, are in a constant state of growth so you are able to periodically reinvent yourself. We are changing by the minute; it is so subtle at times we don't realize it until we look back. It appears the older we get, the faster our birthdays seem to come, but time does not change.

Death Before Your Time

So many people die way ahead of their time, don't be one of them. A life without dreams is a dead life.

The End

Death is a ladder we all must climb at some point. What do you want written on your epitaph? Have you thought about it? If you died today, would others say you lived a purposeful life? What will your dash say?

I first encountered this reality at 12 years of age. A close friend of mine died (RIP Benjamin Okai). He was a very smart guy who stayed on top of his classes all the time. The news of his death cut me like a knife. I didn't know how to come to terms with the fact I was never going to see him again. I wept that night, but little did I know this was just the beginning of the many woes that came along with life. Death is a hard pill to swallow, but it is part of our development and experience in life.

Nails cease to grow when we die.

TWELVE
SMART TOOL

We use our fingernails for countless reasons. If you found a little dried ketchup on your pants, in the absence of a paper towel, you'd use your nails to scrap it off. You'd feel great if you were able to successfully get that dirt off your shirt without a stain. We can use our nails to remove hair from various places. Some might not identify with this but adding a key to a ring or key chain is usually harder without fingernails. Nails are used to scratch an itch and as a tool to scratch off the temporary coverings found on recharge cards and lottery tickets. There were times you couldn't find a toothpick or failed to bring your dental floss, your nail became the perfect tool to remove that piece of meat or popcorn from between your teeth. There are situations where we are desperate for a tool and our nails come in handy.

While these may not be the best use of our nails, you now understand fingernails have endless uses and I'm sure you can think of other examples of using nails as a smart tool. Regardless of who you are, you are gifted with unique abilities and skills. Like nails, you are a smart tool specially crafted for your work.

Nails in a way are like salt, its presence is not really felt until you take it out. Although they are smaller in size, in the grand scheme of things they matter!

Leverage

Our fingernails help us type faster; they are a smart tool in a figurative sense. Having something to use as a leverage gives us a leg up in life. Leverage comes from the word lever and levers are time savers!

When you think of smart tools, what words come to mind? Automation, fast, speed, productivity, effectiveness? It could be all of these and more. We are in the days of mind power not manpower, both are needed but one pays more. It's more like comparing manual to automation! In a few years bots, automation and the likes will take over a lot of manual work. There was an interesting article I read about Bill Gates arguing that robots that take your job should pay taxes. I guess we can use these taxes to advance social welfare for the betterment of citizens.

Smart tools, or having leverage, should not be seen as a substitute for working hard in life, you cannot affect your world by doing the bare minimum. I believe in working smart so don't even bother! However, there are times when we just need to roll up our sleeves or put in the hours and get it done; easy come easy go.

Begin to ask yourself basic questions like "how much time do I have at my disposal to work on my own?" That includes family time, if you have a family, after doing a 9-5 job before retiring to bed. That is where taking advantage of a lever (leverage implied) becomes important. According to basic laws of productivity, you don't have to do everything by yourself.

Creating Wealth - Your Holy Grail to Retirement

I don't know of any billionaire who did it all by themselves without employing the service of others. Could you even imagine me trying to publish this book all by myself. That would mean I have to set up a publishing company or do a self-print. Now, how many copies can I print in a day if I am targeting millions of people? It is simply not worth the hassle. There is no point to doing it all by yourself! This is why we need all the different departments coming together to make a great company and I am not just talking about staffing your areas of weakness.

Amazon® is just one of the many companies who understand this concept; that is why they are doing everything they can to lift the heavy weights for you. Think of Amazon products like Relay, Drop Shipping and Merch among others. I don't have to learn how to do video editing to get my video intro when I can pay less than $50 on Fiverr to get it done in no time. Additionally, I don't have to learn how to design a logo. Even if I could do it, what are the chances it will come out better than leveraging the services of an expert. Even in academia, I recall Chegg, Course Hero, Quizlet and the likes were all life savers when I was in school. I recall renting a couple of textbooks from Chegg which were much cheaper than if I were to buy them outright. You simply need leverage, we all do, and it is in our best interest. You get the concept?

This leads me to wealth creation where the same principles apply. Use leverage! Warren Buffett said, "*If you don't find a way to make money while you sleep, you will work until you die."* From listening and talking to financial advisers, wealth creation, in my opinion, takes an average of 5-10 years minimum to be in a comfortable place depending on the goals you set.

Wealth is not an event, but a process. M. J. DeMarco, author of *The Millionaire Fastlane*, says it best - *"Wealth is not a road, but a road trip."* One of the ways we can all create wealth according to this book, is to grow money trees (this is explained below). Have you heard of the saying "Money does not grow on trees?" Well, according to DeMarco, it can if you plant trees that grow money. In other words, build the right systems to support a consistent cash flow. Money trees, as indicated by DeMarco, require periodic support or maintenance. Nonetheless, they are business systems that can survive on their own. Growing money trees includes, but is not limited to, the following in no particular order.

Build money trees:
- o   RENTAL SYSTEMS – Real estate properties, licensing (like music licensing).
- o   DISTRIBUTION SYSTEMS - Like Amazon, middleman jobs.
- o   SOFTWARE – SAAS, Digital Asset.
- o   CONTENT SYSTEMS – Book writing, YouTube, an online course.

Another key lesson he talked about is to switch from a consumer to a producer mindset. Let me expound on the producer mindset a bit. From childhood our minds have been programmed unconsciously to be consumers. For instance, we are constantly asking people, "What do you want for your birthday?" "What would you like when you are done with school?" "What would you do if you won the mega million lottery?" There is nothing wrong with having a blast or celebrations, but if you want to become rich then you have to switch from this type of consumer mindset to a producer mindset.

Celebrate your kids, they deserve every bit of it. But they don't have to suffer because you did; they don't have to work hard because you worked hard. They will work hard, but not your type of "hard work" because you have given them a leg up. They don't have to start at the bottom, because you have laid the foundation and given them a step up, not a handout. Personally, I like to distance myself from people who have such a toxic mindset. It is better to share your experience, than to expect people to suffer just because you suffered. There is no beauty or admiration in that. Each process we soften makes it better for all of us in the eco-system, as we are all interconnected.

Let's begin to change the narrative. Ask your children questions such as, "By the time you are 18 years old, what do you hope to have produced?" "What dream do you wish to have birthed in this world?" That is a producer mindset. Anytime you buy something new or visit a beautiful place, let your mind go on a cruise and enjoy the wonders of imagination, think about the possibilities. How was this produced? Can I do this too? How? Unless it is not an area of interest for you. This is understandable, it is better to master one thing rather than attempt to be a jack of all trades and master of none.

Living a Productive Life

Begin to think of things you do repeatedly on a daily, weekly, or monthly basis. Is there a way you can automate any of it or cut it out of your time? Would you rather have more time or sacrifice your time? Can you afford to let someone else take care of your lawn? Then go ahead and pay for it to free up your day, use that as a leverage to invest quality time in something else. That is why people specialize in different areas and industries.

Discovering Your Zone

It is important to discover your zone. Are you a producer, a consumer or both. Most people are consumers, but they will gravitate towards what gives them value. Let value guide you and don't hold back from giving your best, because even with your best, it is only a matter of time before creative disruptors step in and if you're not diligent, they will overtake you.

Fruit Buyers

Everyone needs food to survive, but a fruit buyer mindset is one who gets excited about new releases. What they have may be working well, but they are constantly looking for and buying the latest and greatest. If you can afford to pay cash and don't have to borrow there is nothing wrong with making the purchase. Still, everything should be done in moderation. This is a typical consumer mindset. A fruit buyer can become a fruit seller.

Fruit Sellers

Fruit sellers buy fruit with the intention of selling it. These would be akin to being the middleman in Amazon. They buy and sell fruit they don't produce. If you can build a great infrastructure around it, this zone has the potential to bring a lot of revenue since there are more consumers than producers in this world.

Apple and Google Play stores are also examples of fruit sellers. They don't have to produce everything; they provide the platform for sellers.

Seed Buyers

Seed buyers are the companies and people with a growth mindset. For a company such as Apple, the seed they purchase may be the acquisition of a competing company. But the greatest seed any company can have is their human capital. The real seed buyers are conscious of their intent.

Seed Sellers

Seed sellers refers to those who sell things such as ideas. They may be seen on shows like Shark Tank pitching their business plan to investors. Seed sellers have creative mindsets and may also buy from other seed buyers to sell. Others may merge with seed sellers to sell. If they are savvy enough, they can build an umbrella for multiple businesses, maintaining a share in the concepts (businesses) they sell. Seed sellers are not afraid of losing a seed because they know their mind is fruity. However, they must be careful to ensure the right non-disclosure agreements are signed before pitching ideas to others.

In any of these zones, if there are opportunities to leverage, don't hesitate to use it to your advantage in order to level up.

Home Association

Homeowner's associations, commonly referred to as HOAs, are self-governing organizations consisting of residents living in the same community who pay fees annually to maintain the common spaces. Those serving on the HOA board, or volunteering in some capacity, can also make new friends. It is a great way to not only build a community, but you never know who your neighbor down the street might be. Imagine bumping into a mentor you have always admired in your neighborhood; they may have just moved in a few weeks ago, or maybe they have always been there and you did not know.

This is not to say go and take advantage of people living in the same community as you. It also provides an opportunity for your kids to play with other kids in the community. This is one way for them to develop their social skills and escape boredom in the house. I can remember a time my next-door neighbor helped me set up a baby gate for our stairs. It took him no time at all, and I didn't have to pay a handy man. It is all about leverage, I am sure you have many examples as well.

Online Community

We can use technology as a leverage to build great professional and personal branded communities online. Don't be deceived by people with huge followings on social media. A follower does not automatically translate to loyalty to one's brand. I have read of stories where some social influencers organized a meet and greet and nobody showed up. Virtual following has its pros and cons. Understand the science behind it so you can properly use it as a "leverage."

At the same time, you can build real connections. It is always good to start with people you know to build a solid online community; people who will not pull the plug on you for whatever reason. One of the differences is usually it will be a private group "hosted" on social media, or built from scratch, as opposed to public groups on social media where everybody can join.

Information and key contacts can be easily shared because there is a common interest. Another advantage is you have greater control and security if you actually own the community, a website, or app you built from scratch. This way you aren't afraid of YouTube or Facebook deactivating your account for going against a rule. You make the decisions and you call the shots, as agreed by the community. The platform is community driven. You have a better opportunity to generate leads thereby increasing your conversion rate drastically. Furthermore, customers will appreciate your differentiation from the market or from other options. Who doesn't like customization? We all do. This is how many stay on the winning side these days.

THIRTEEN
STAY IN A POSITIVE ENVIRONMENT

Did you know increasing your water intake can improve dry fingernails? Stay in a positive environment, connect with people who will keep watering, challenging, and developing you. It is no secret that high impact performers or leaders choose education over entertainment. The determination to be educated will push you to stay in a positive environment.

Growing up I recall my father visiting one of the schools I attended to inquire about my performance. Something the teachers said to my father, which he relayed to me, has stuck with me over the years. They told him as long as I continued to hang around with Dennis Daddey and Emmanuel Amoako I'd do well academically. And he was right, those guys all did well on their final exams and went on to some of the top universities in the country. What did they see in these guys? Success, just like failure is predictable. Staying in the right environment, with the right people, is key to growth.

Why do some things resonate with you and others don't? Because we think and operate on frequencies. Our frequencies or energies are more aligned with what's going to happen in the future, as opposed to what's happening right now. So stay away from environments that do not challenge you. Entrepreneur Robert Kiyosaki said, *"If you own a butcher shop, don't hire vegetarians. To hire the right people, you have to let the wrong people go."* Anything that pulls you down should go. They will spoil your business because you are going in opposite directions.

FOURTEEN
COLOR

Add some color to your life. Aren't you tired of wearing dull colors? This is not to say go and polish your nails red or blue, but you can if that is what you want. The point is you need color in your life.

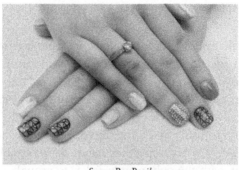

Source: RoseBnails

Be joyful, get some life, get some fresh air, take a vacation, live your best life. Here are some of my favorite quotes on color.

"Art washes away from the soul
the dust of everyday life."
- Pablo Picasso

This quote by Picasso hits me hard. We all know art is beautiful, art is colorful, and I cannot say it any better than the way Picasso said it. Indeed, it washes away the dust of everyday life.

"To me, beauty and makeup and color is like the
finishing touch on everything."
- Marc Jacobs

"Nature always wears the colors of the spirit."
- Ralph Waldo Emerson

"If everyone would look for that uniqueness
then we would have a very colorful world."
- Michael Schenker

Michael Schenker also nailed it, I tell people all the time, there is a particular color or element unique to you that the world is looking for before you exit. The world is waiting for you to paint that idea, to color the sky and blanket it with your thoughts. As a matter of fact, let's go ahead and state this affirmation.

> _Affirmation_: Thoughts are like clouds in the sky. I refuse to give up and I am going to blanket the skies with what's inside of me and I will be sure to make it colorful.

If you don't use your colors, nature will find a different person who will and we will lose them. Isn't it disappointing when you conceived an idea only to see it come to pass through someone else later? You missed an opportunity because you didn't act. I have given this a lot of thought and I feel it's almost as if the universe blesses us with specific ideas that hit the world at the same time just seeking thinkers, believers and most importantly doers to pick it up. Some call it an "aha moment," some call it an epiphany, some call it eureka. It's the same thing, just different words.

> _"Try to be a rainbow in someone's cloud."_
> - Maya Angelou

This quote is one of the best lines I have ever heard. Don't you love a rainbow when it appears after rain? Why do we love it? Because it is colorful. So be unapologetically you; be the light that shines in a dark world, be that rainbow.

> _"The purest and most thoughtful minds are_
> _those which love color the most."_
> - John Ruskin

> _"Life is like a rainbow. You need both rain and_
> _sun to make its colors appear."_
> - Unknown

Color is the spark. This might be worth repeating because you are certainly not the first, and won't be the last, in the area of the profession you find yourself pursuing. However, after all is said and done, one thing is assured -

add color to your craft if you want to stand out. This is what will separate you from the rest.

Your color or uniqueness might not appear big to you until you express it only to your amazement. What you call small, that little bit of humor can make all the difference in people's life. People will only remember you for how you made them feel after sharing that thought and adding color to their life.

A woman stepped from her brand-new SUV and entered a restaurant looking so depressed. I opened the door for her and guess what she said? "You made my day." My small act of service added color to her life, so don't ignore the urge to add color where it is needed, especially when it is needed. Saying a simple thank you, doing good and being nice, all add color to people's lives.

Years ago I saw Ledith, a subject matter expert (SME) colleague of mine, wearing two rings on two different fingers. I didn't even think what I said was funny, but it made a world of difference to her and she couldn't help but laugh out loud. I was like, "Ledith! Are you married to two people?" Remember that tiny bit of humor could make an impact. Evaluate your thoughts first and watch what you say.

I also believe color is the divine stamp that announces to the world that our time has come. Usain Bolt is not the first runner in the world, but he was clever enough to add color, or his own signature, to his craft. The signature alone has garnered him many deals all over the world.

Source: Usainbolt.com

So, adding color to your skill has a way of announcing you. It speaks in this regard - what we have been rehearsing, preparing behind the scenes, is fully baked and ready to serve it to the world. In other words, it makes a statement to the world that there is a new guy on the block that you have to check out. He is doing something out of the ordinary. Out of the ordinary doesn't necessarily mean it is new, because really there is nothing new under the sun, but check him out because he has separated himself from the norm. Imitation makes what was once original, lose its color. So, when you add color, it makes you stand out.

Who is the color in your life? Better still, who are the colors in your life?

Adding color does not mean to complicate things. Leonardo da Vinci said, *"Simplicity is the ultimate sophistication."*

Do you know someone who is always trying to be deep? Let your depth show in your simplicity; make it look so simple until they try it.

I hope we are all able to say at the tail end of our lives that…

"I have led a pretty colorful life."
- Corey Feldman

FIFTEEN
LEADERSHIP

When you look at your fingernails, one of them stands taller than the rest because it lies on the longest finger – the middle finger. But being the longest does not necessarily make you a leader. Appearances can be deceptive. When it comes to your hand, the thumb is the leader. The thumb, or better still the thumb nail, is separate from the rest and that's what leadership is about. Typically larger than the others also, the thumbnail can easily touch all the other nails. In our analogy, this could infer being an effective communicator. When it comes to communication, the thumb could be the one networking and pulling the team together. You would have to stand out in terms of virtue, skill, intelligence and such in order to lead the rest. Think about it. If I am in the same class with you and I consider myself better because I excel in all the subjects and you don't, why would I come to you for lecture notes when it should be the other way around. People will travel far and wide to see others because of their higher perceived value.

Additionally, the thumb on which the thumbnail rests not only stands out, but it is also indispensable because you cannot hold anything with a firm grip without the thumb. Also, when you make a fist you will discover all the other fingers go under the thumb which signifies authority, headship, and leadership (I will discuss servant leadership in the coming section). This is not to be confused with people using their authority to lord over others. That is not what true leadership is about. Leaders exist to serve. Our world, now more than ever, is at the mercy of leadership. John C. Maxwell said, *"Everything begins and ends with leadership."* In this chapter, the thumb will represent leadership. Like I said before, I believe there is a leader in all of us. This is briefly what I have to say about leadership.

Leadership Defined

In my mind, leadership can be likened to ministry. A genuine ministry of any type is born out of pure passion, willingness of heart, a clear conscious and the desire to help or serve others. The keyword here is SERVE. Serving comes from the greatest leader of all time, in my opinion and you don't have to agree, but his name is Jesus Christ. He said, "Whoever wants to be a leader among you must be your servant." He took a bottom-up approach. You have to reach down to lift people up with you.

Today, servant leadership has become a thing however this was a quality Jesus demonstrated on a consistent basis almost 2000 years ago (he started his ministry at age 30). He also said, "I came to serve, not to be served". The goal of serving means just that, serving humanity. Serving with a clear conscious, not with ulterior motives to get fame or money. If money and notoriety comes as a result of your service then so be it, but that is not the goal.

One of my favorite thoughts on leadership comes from John C. Maxwell. I grew reading his books which helped shape my mind. He said, *"Leadership is INFLUENCE, nothing more, nothing less."*

Another one of my favorite quotes is by Martin Luther King Jr. He said, *"Everybody can be great, because everyone can serve."* A heart of service is a rare commodity, but whether we like it or not, the genuine way to the top is through service to humanity.

Unfortunately, I don't subscribe to Peter Drucker's definition of leadership - *"The only definition of a leader is someone who has followers."* By his definition, the mother nursing our future president would be disqualified because she has no one following her, irrespective of all the values and principles she is instilling in this young boy or girl. It takes a leader to birth a leader. Likewise, men influencing their home environment positively, inspiring their kids, and doing all it takes to put food on the table would not be considered leadership. Women who juggle a dozen things at once to keep the home together, and women serving in different capacities without followers but constantly demonstrating exemplary leadership would be disqualified. The list is endless. I appreciate all the work Peter has done, but this definition is perhaps too simple, for lack of a better word.

In actuality, you can have followers who end up sabotaging you because they never liked you to begin with. There are so many people out there with no titles and no one following them, yet they are leading every day in different capacities to the point where some even put their lives on the line. You may even know of people who demonstrated leadership qualities that inspired a whole generation with no followers until they became popular for their actions. There are people writing books and poetry who have no followers, yet they are changing lives every day.

Leadership does not only have to be in speech, it can take on other forms as well. We say tears are unspoken words, well, leadership can be silent too yet it speaks because it comes from the heart. Actions are loudspeakers, so let your actions as a leader speak for you. I hope your actions inspire someone to have hope in humanity, to believe that all is not lost. Elon Musk said, *"We have to be excited about the future!"* And I agree.

Subject You

When it comes to leadership, the only subject you really ought to know first is you. What does this mean?

Well, to become a leader you must help yourself by growing. Subject You – is the most important subject you will ever learn because you are in charge! Whether you fail or succeed is on you, so take the pen of the story of your life and write it yourself. YES, it's a life-long process as we are changing every day. Your foundation, values and knowledge base of knowing who you are has to be established at some point, but this doesn't stop you from adding to it or discovering more about you. You need to know your strengths and weaknesses. This will guide your decisions on what to say yes or no to, to avoid wasting precious time. Knowing yourself requires constant self-consciousness, having a growth mindset, and being emotionally intelligent.

Think about it, if you don't love and accept yourself how do you preach to others to embrace who they are? Knowing yourself is a confidence booster. There are people who speak and it's just empty words because their words don't carry any weight. Then there are others who speak and you just know they are speaking life to you becomes it comes from a place of deeper understanding. These are people who are not only experts in their respective domains but have a strong sense of self-worth. So, focus on growing yourself, sit down, lock yourself in a room until you discover the most important subject in the world – The Subject You!

"Before you are a leader, success is all about growing yourself. When you become a leader, success is all about growing others."
- Jack Welch

Suffering Unmasked

Kahlil Gibran, a Lebanese author popularly known for his book *The Prophet* says, *"Your joy is your sorrow unmasked."* The painful truth is, when you look at our greatest heroes they have one thing in common, for the most part, and that is suffering. This is something I learned from Robin Sharma, *"The greatest ones suffered the most"*. Uneasy lies the head that wears the crown.
Growing pains are not peculiar to a select few, they just come with growing.

Leadership is NOT

Leadership is not about ranks or titles.

> *"Become the kind of leader that people would follow voluntarily; even if you had no title or position."*
> - Brian Tracy

Leadership is an attitude, not a position. That is not to say there is anything wrong with positions or having a C-level title. I believe in honoring authority, so let's not water down positions, titles, or authority especially when we have the right people in power. However, all of us are leaders in our own right - one can lead from the bottom, middle, or the top. When we limit leadership to only those with titles, it causes people to betray the leader that lies within them. Again, I 100% agree with Robin Sharma, who in his book *The Leader Who Had No Title* assures anyone can lead without a title. While the world says you have to be a prime minister, or a president, or a pastor, or a chairman, or hold an MBA or PhD, or be a billionaire or CEO to be significant, I don't agree. Do you really think you need a title to lead?

You can actually be a leader and lose your sense of leadership in a given scenario.

Let's consider the use of leadership in the following cases.

Leadership: Case One

Here's a true story. In my undergrad studies, one of my lecturers left his classroom one day and saw an empty water bottle on the floor. He thought it was beneath his rank to pick it up and put it in the trash. While he was still contemplating this, the chancellor of the university, someone with far greater authority than he, happened to walk by. The chancellor saw the water bottle on the floor and immediately picked it up and trashed it. There was a restroom nearby, so he went inside afterward to wash his hands and walked on without saying a word. This is a leader who demonstrated he hasn't lost himself because of a title. As Gandhi said, *"The best way to find yourself is to lose yourself in the service of others."*

This chancellor (Professor Stephen Adei) gave up his title in essence, he lost himself at that moment. He could have said, oh that's not my job, the janitor will come for it in due time, but he didn't. I believe he demonstrated not just service but true humility. Such a leader is the type that would not lord his leadership over his subordinates. That is failed leadership my friend! Wherever you find yourself, in a mosque, church, company, firm, or NGO, be sure to serve and not expect anything in return.

Leadership: Case Two

I heard a similar story shared by a real estate mogul named, Nana Kwame Bediako, CEO of Wonda World Estates, in a podcast I was listening to some time ago. He shared an experience he had while driving with his family. One of his kids threw something out of the window of his car. Seeing this, a man got out of his vehicle, picked it up, placed it in the trash and went back to his car. What he was saying was - I value my country more than my ego, pride, or title. That is what I call a leader with no title. It is not about accolades and having a huge following; those who are in the limelight as well as the unknown folks can all lead.

Positive Communication in Leadership

Learn to communicate hard things in a pleasant way, with emotional intelligence, or else you might lose your leadership. Use the "sandwich approach" if you have to. The sandwich approach is one of the effective ways to chastise people. It wraps negative feedback in praise. The dialogue begins by offering a positive comment first, proceeded by correcting whatever you did wrong, followed by a final encouragement using appreciative and positive words to lift you up.

Intentional Leadership

We can all be intentional in the way we lead and the rewards of leading with intentionality are simply immeasurable. Following are three easy things we can all adopt.

NEVER TALK DOWN TO PEOPLE: A leader seeks opportunities to uplift people and not the other way around.

BELIEVE AND SEE VALUE IN PEOPLE: This should be done on a consistent basis, so be on the lookout.

GIVING UNCONDITIONAL LOVE: This love seeks ways to appreciate people even in the smallest things. Learn to touch people's hearts before you touch their hands. If people over time perceive you to be a taker, and not a giver, they may push back when being told to do something, or decline to give something without getting anything in return.

I have some questions for you.

When was the last time you bought a book for your leader just to show appreciation for the things you have learned from their leadership?

When was the last time you ordered a birthday cake for a loved one?

When was the last time you called or texted someone just to say "I love you"? One night I sent such a text message to a couple of people and the responses were overwhelming. One of them texted back by saying she had been waiting for it. A sense of belonging is something every one of us appreciates. In the end, only love matters. That is the summation of it all. So do not admire quietly. If you love something about someone, tell them. I am not a prophet of doom, but for all you know that might be the last time you will ever see or hear from them. So, get on and do it.

The Unbiased Leader

There are great leaders all over the world, but some are only good at meeting the needs of their own race. Some are biased towards other races, and some just don't know how to relate to other cultures. My advice for a leader who seeks to break this barrier is to travel and experience other cultures, if you can afford it. This can boost creativity in leadership. You get to see what other leaders are doing elsewhere.

Another alternative to traveling is to read a wide variety of material. Reading the right materials can go a long way to inspire one's mind, it could take you on endless travels and escapades around the universe.

FUN FACTS

In an article entitled *How the 5 Fingers Got Their Names*[7], Andrew LaSane shares an anecdote around the naming origins of our fingers.

The first finger is the thumb, or pollex in medical terms. Originates from the Proto-Indo-European term "tum" meaning to swell or the swollen one.

Followed by the index finger (forefinger) which comes from the Latin word "indico", meaning to point out. Obviously, this is the finger we use to point or show people the way.

The middle finger does just that, it sits in the middle (digitus medius manus) and is the tallest or longest of all. As such, it's also known as the long or tall finger.

The ring finger has an interesting history. Egyptians are believed to have made up the theory that the fourth finger had a vein called the "lover's vein" which supposedly connects to the heart. Romans bought into this theory as well, that if a man truly held a woman's heart he would follow the gospel of Beyoncé and "put a ring on it." This explains why it is still practiced today.

The little finger, or pinkie, is the smallest finger (digitus minimus manus). The Scottish and Dutch languages term something small as "pinkie" or "pink" and so that's how the little finger got its name.

---

[7]Andrew LaSane, How the 5 Fingers Got Their Names, Mental Floss, 1 Mar 2016 (www.mentalfloss.com/article/74308/how-5-fingers-got-their-names).

CONCLUSION

"Our deepest fear is not that we are inadequate. Our deepest fear is that we are powerful beyond measure. It is our light, not our darkness that most frightens us."
- Marianne Williamson

At the end of the day, you need to stand for something. There is nothing profitable about shrinking so other people won't feel insecure around you. Let your light shine bright evermore. When we do this, we unconsciously give other people permission to do the same. As we are liberated from our own fear, our presence automatically liberates others.

Finally, let's learn to be thankful in our pursuit of happiness. Learn to share what we have with others, learn to direct the accolades to our audience. Be thankful. That's what real leaders do; they acknowledge others because they know we rise by lifting others.

Many receive lessons and advice in life, but it profits only the wise. Let's take a cue from our nails and stay wise.

Thank you for taking time to read this book.

REFERENCES

"25 Fascinating Facts About Fingernails." *Desert Hand and Physical Therapy.* n.d.

Academy, Kahn. *Where do our nails and hair come from?* n.d.

Ballantyne, Adrian. "Moment #15: Giving up not an option for John Stephen Akhwari." *Fox Sports.* n.d. https://www.foxsports.com.au/olympic-games/moment-15-giving-up-not-an-option-for-john-stephen-akhwari/news-story/60947bd56b387d7eec8d917db9f611b3.

Branson, Richard. *Richard Branson Funded His First Business at 16 for Less Than $2,000.* n.d.

"Butterfly Metamorphosis Shot with iPhone4S." n.d.

Digangi, Christine. *Americans are Dying with an Average of $62,000 of Debt.* March 22, 2017.

Dweck, Carol. "The Power of Yet." n.d.

Graham, Billy. *On Technology and Faith.* n.d.

Herdieckerhoff, Elena. "The Gentle Power of Highly Sensitive People." n.d.

"How A Caterpillar Becomes A Butterfly." n.d.

LaSane, Eric. *How the 5 Fingers Got their Names.* March 1, 2016.

"Life Cycle of A Frog: From Tadpole to Frog." n.d.

"Lobster Removing His Shell Amazing Video." *Desert Hand and Physical Therapy.* n.d.

"Maasai Chases a Lian Eating His Cow." n.d.

Myers, Louise. *Colorful Quotes.* December 14, 2022.

O'Connor, Amy. *When Babies Start Growing Hair, Skin and Nails.* June 22, 2021.

Planet, Human. "Stealing Meat from Lions." n.d.

Reid, David. *The Digital Broker's Playbook*. New York, NY: Charles Michael
    Publishing, 2021.

Saxe, John Godfrey. *The Blind Men and an Elephant*. New York, NY:
    McGraw Hill, 1963.

Smartphone Addiction Statistics. January 23, 2023.
    https://www.slicktext.com/blog/2019/10/smartphone-addiction-
    statistics/.

Author's Biography

Charles is the CEO of LionsMatrix: The Ultimate Growth Matrix. He is a Certified Product Owner by profession with a decade's worth of work as an IT professional spanning across different skillset and domains. He has had the privilege of consulting for Fortune 500 companies and experienced different leadership styles in his journey. He is also a speaker, Meaning Maker, MBA graduate, entrepreneur, a recipient of "Citizens Award" from Statewide ITPA while working at TN Department of Environment & Conservation and an author of the new book *Lessons from Nails*.

When not writing, he can be found reading, listening to podcasts, hiking, site seeing and traveling. His mission statement is to "inspire humankind" through his writings. He is based in Atlanta, Georgia together with his wife and kids. If you would like to stay inspired or connect, check out his website www.lionsmatrix.com.